WEATHERCASTING

To our parents

Introduction

No one will deny the importance of the weather. To the community as a whole, it holds the key to economic prosperity or disaster. To the individual, it means health or sickness, happiness or discomfort. But how much do we know about this important element of our life? As Benjamin Franklin aptly remarked: "Some people are weatherwise, but most are otherwise."

This is an age of "do-it-yourself" in the very best American tradition of self-reliance. What to do about the weather? Much is being done now by the Government with its organized weather services and current experiments in rain-making and weather control. But these are large-scale operations far beyond the scope of an individual.

So what can you do about the weather? As outlined in the following pages, you can build your own weather station; and from your own backyard you can take systematic observations and watch the pageant of the skies pass overhead. You can study the principles of atmospheric behavior and make your own forecasts. In time you will become weatherwise and can then apply this knowledge to the greater health, happiness, and prosperity of your family and community.

David M. Ludlum
Editor, *Weatherwise* Magazine

Preface

The aim of *Weathercasting* is to furnish material to the amateur meteorologist which will help him get a good start in a fascinating hobby. The authors have included information, particularly in those sections on obtaining weather map data and on construction of instruments, which was gleaned the "hard way" over a period of time.

Thanks are given to Dr. David M. Ludlum of *Weatherwise Magazine* for his helpful suggestions and for permission to use some of the data on construction of weather instruments, published earlier in *Weatherwise* and written by Charles Laird.

The United States Weather Bureau generously allowed the writers to use information pertaining to weather map construction and forecasting. Credit is given in each instance where official Weather Bureau photographs are used.

Photographs of some standard weather instruments were supplied by Instruments Corp. and Bendix-Friez, and our thanks go to them also.

Charles and Ruth Laird

Table of Contents

1. INTRODUCTION 1

2. OBSERVING 6

3. FORECASTING 44

4. INSTRUMENTS 110

INDEX 153

1

Introduction

All of us are amateur meteorologists, to some degree. Yot most of us, as we talk about the weather, put on our overcoats, take them off, or scan the skies for signs of rain before going on a picnic, probably don't think of ourselves as such. The degree of proficiency reached by the amateur meteorologist depends on his enthusiasm. Chances are if you think it's going to rain, and still go on that picnic because a summer shower on the baked beans enhances your enjoyment of the outing, you're an enthusiastic amateur. Many cartoons have been drawn on the subject of rain at a Weather

Bureau picnic. It might be the Weather Bureau planned its annual outing with that in mind!

Just as there are hobbyists who devote hours to amateur radio and model railroading, so are there men and women who plan their leisure time around meteorology. The soup may grow cold and the baby get wetter, but your blood pressure will go down and your appreciation of the wonders of nature will rise, as you watch the progress of a summer thunderstorm.

To the true amateur meteorologist, the thrills of Barnum and Bailey pale by comparison to that still moment just before the first raindrop slaps against the windowpane, and the lightning moves closer as the storm passes overhead. The works of Corot can never recapture the beauty of that strip of lighted sky encircling the dark cloud directly above that is pouring forth its rain. Such a memory is magnificent proof of God's wonders—life-giving rain, a promise of sun, and the earth welcoming both. Weather even points up the security of home. Who hasn't snuggled deeper under the covers, with a late fall rain beating a pleasant tattoo against the old tin roof!

What is an amateur? Webster says he is "one who cultivates a particular pursuit, study, or science, from taste, without pursuing it professionally; also a dabbler."

Amateur meteorology is a big subject, so weather

hobbyists may take their pick of many phases, and dabble or cultivate, as suits their fancy. Some are interested in observing the weather, noting its changing patterns and effects, and making notes, graphs and tables of weather conditions. They're the weather statisticians, piling up records and working out averages. If you think it's hot today, they may say, it's nothing compared to July 25, 1941, when the mercury soared to 112.

Many amateur meteorologists are interested in forecasting. They may do it by observing conditions at their particular location, or they can get a more general picture of the weather, on a national or international scale, from national weather maps and short- and long-wave radio reports. Methods of doing this will be explained later in this book.

One of the most interesting phases of amateur meteorology, especially to anyone with a mechanical frame of mind, is the use of weather instruments and construction of recording and indicating devices. While a few amateurs may be able to build such devices without any help, most will need some instruction. Toward that end, the last section of this book is devoted to instruments of the home workshop variety. If you haven't spent much time at putting things together, don't discard the idea as impossible for you. Even a simple wind vane, whittled from a shingle and swinging on a nail driven in the top of a post, is a valuable aid to the amateur. You can make the whole thing in ten minutes, and have the fun of watching something you've made work.

Do you like to draw? Then maybe your forte is working up attractive base maps on which to plot weather movement.

The amateur photographer (or professional, for that matter) has an unlimited field in the photography of clouds and other weather phenomena. Some friends of ours have gone in for cloud photography in a big way, and have taken beautiful color photographs of clouds, rainbows, sunsets, et cetera.

The amateur meteorologist doesn't have to sit in a little cobwebby niche and hide his light under a bushel. As in other fields, contributions to meteorology have been made by amateurs. There's always a chance that you, with your weather plotting and figuring and head-scratching, will come up with something everyone else has missed, either in the field of forecasting or instrument research.

Some ways of combining amateur meteorology with other hobbies have been suggested above. There are other ways too. For example, radio amateurs are interested in weather from a propagation standpoint. And they can use their talent in the electronic and mechanical field to build weather instruments. Did you know that some modern weather instruments use radio tubes in their construction? Perhaps you can figure out a way to use transistors, a new device in electronics.

If you're convinced that yours is more than a casual interest in weather, you're probably asking, How much do I need in the way of equipment? The first thought with most of us in taking up a hobby is the strain on the old pocketbook. There's good news on that score. You can start with nothing but your eyes, a pencil and pad and your oldest pair of bluejeans and blue denim shirt. You don't even need the pencil and pad. The eyes are necessary, the pants and shirt optional. You can go out now and take a look at the sky and see in which direction smoke is traveling. Then, tomorrow at the same time, take another look and see how much change has taken place in 24 hours. You can say, "See, yesterday it was cloudy and the wind was coming from the south. Today it's clear and the wind is from the northwest." In a sense, dear reader, you are now an amateur meteorologist.

Amateur meteorology as a hobby has no limitations. You can do it casually, like the observer in the bluejeans. Or you can have every instrument in the book for local observation, plus radio code or teletype printing devices to give you a continuous picture of weather on an international scale.

5

2

Observing

Farmers, ranchers and others who spend a great deal of time outdoors get very well acquainted with clouds and weather and even become quite adept at forecasting future conditions for their particular area.

As an amateur meteorologist, it is important to put weather observing on a semiscientific basis, by using a pattern or form for such observations. That doesn't mean you should enter weather conditions on a ruled pad at exactly 8 A.M. today and then forget all about the weather until 8 o'clock tomorrow morning. Keep a good watch on the weather at all times and take

6

down notes whenever you can. A glance out of the window once in a while, even during working hours, will enable you to note significant changes.

It is a good idea to have a regular form for entering your weather observations, one observation to be made, perhaps, in the morning and another at a convenient time in the evening—or more per day, if you have the time. For purposes of working up temperature averages, pressure trends, et cetera, the ideal method is to have a definite time for making the observations. But you might also leave a space on your form for noting significant weather activity that occurs at other times during the day.

The observation forms used in some professional services show data entered in about the following manner. (Of course, you can make entries in any order you please. This is *your* hobby.)

> *Clouds: Types, estimated heights, direction and speed of movement, amount of sky covered*
>
> *Visibility: How far can you see in a horizontal direction*
>
> *Weather: Rain, snow, thunderstorm, fog or any other weather phenomena*
>
> *Temperature*
>
> *Dew point or relative humidity*

7

Wind direction

Wind velocity

Barometric pressure

Amount of rain or snow since last observation

Maximum and minimum temperatures since last observation

Remarks: Data on significant weather occurrences since your previous observation

Figure 1 shows a sample form. You might use a similar one for a start, but as your knowledge of weather observing increases you will probably want to incorporate your own ideas on a form of your own.

When you have decided what you want your observation form to include, you may want to print a number of copies to save the work of ruling a new one out by hand at the end of each week or month. One of the cheapest methods of reproducing copies is by the hectograph process.

Available at most stationery stores is a material called hectograph gelatine. It is a semisolid substance and comes in a sealed metal can. This substance is heated until it is soft enough to flow. It is then poured into a shallow pan, of a size somewhat larger than the forms you expect to reproduce, and allowed to cool to its original consistency. In the meantime, you

8

Time	Clouds Amount, Type, Dir., Height	Visi-bility	Weather	Temp.	Dew Pt.	Wind Dir.	Wind Vel.	Baro-meter	Rain or Snow Since Last ob.	Remarks
.										

Fig. 1 Example of observation form.

can draw out the observation form you have decided on, using hectograph ink or copying pencil of the Ditto type. Then carefully flatten out your inked or pencil copy, face down, on the hectograph gelatine surface, leaving it there several seconds. With the master copy thus set, you can then make as many as several hundred copies of the form, by carefully laying blank sheets of paper on the gelatine surface and allowing the imprint to transfer to the under surface of the paper. Complete instructions are printed on each hectograph can.

There are, of course, many methods of reproduction possible—Mimeograph, lithography and even regular printing press process. But whichever you choose, don't have too many forms printed at the start. You may change your mind about what you want to enter as you gain weather experience.

Fig. 2 Cirrus clouds. (*U.S. Weather Bureau; H. T. Floreen*)

Clouds

Observing clouds is a very interesting and important part of amateur weather work. Types of clouds, their heights, direction of movement, and so forth, are ever-changing and have a significant effect on present and future weather.

Weather services throughout the world have agreed on a standard classification for cloud forms. These forms, and their abbreviations, include the following: Cirrus (Ci), cirrostratus (Cs), cirrocumulus (Cc), altostratus (As), altocumulus (Ac), stratocumulus

10

Fig. 3 Cirrocumulus predominating, associated with cirrus. (*U.S. Army, Photo Section; Lake Charles, La., Flying School*)

(Sc), nimbostratus (Ns), cumulus (Cu), cumulonimbus (Cb) and stratus (St). Sometimes the prefix "fracto" is attached to a cloud form to indicate it is broken or shredded by wind, i.e., fractostratus (Fs) or fractocumulus (Fc). Cloud classification is quite simple, once you get acquainted with the general

11

types, some of which are shown in photographs on these pages (Figures 2 through 11).

Of course, you don't have to become familiar with these scientific classifications for clouds if you don't care to. This is your hobby, and maybe you're not the eager-beaver type. You might simply wish to note Clear, Partly Cloudy or Cloudy on your form. Or you can enlarge on such entries by adding Dark Clouds, Low Clouds, and others.

For those who want to become familiar with the regular classifications, we will describe them briefly on the following pages. For a more thorough under-

Fig. 4 Thick altostratus clouds near the horizon, thickening to nimbostratus overhead. (*U.S. Weather Bureau; C. F. Brooks*)

Fig. 5 Altocumulus clouds. (*U.S. Weather Bureau;*
A. J. Reed)

standing, and for descriptions of cloud types not included here, the U.S. Weather Bureau offers a number of publications on the subject. A list of these
publications may be obtained by writing to the Superintendent of Documents, Washington 25, D.C., and
asking for Price List 48, "Weather, Astronomy and
Meteorology."

Let us start with the main general types of clouds:
Cirrus clouds are the high, filmy kind. They sometimes
begin to form after a period of fair weather, and may
be forerunners of a change to stormy conditions. The
familiar mare's-tails and mackerel sky are types of cir-

13

Fig. 6 Altocumulus clouds formed by a spreading out of the tops of cumulus. (*U.S. Weather Bureau*)

rus formations. Cirrus clouds which have developed into a sheet-like, spreading formation are called cirrostratus. Sometimes cirrostratus clouds will cover the whole sky. Another cirrus development is cirrocumulus—high, woolly puffs of clouds, which may cover a wide area. Sometimes the tops of cumulonimbus clouds spread out and have a cirrus-like appearance. Formerly called false cirrus, the correct scientific term is cirrusnothus. There is really nothing false about them.

The prefix "alto" is used in the description of clouds. These are clouds of a stratus or cumulus nature at a

Fig. 7 Nimbostratus clouds associated with a cold front. (*U.S. Weather Bureau; John O. Ward*)

Fig. 8 Fair weather cumulus. (*U.S. Weather Bureau; H. T. Floreen*)

medium altitude. Common medium-altitude types are altostratus, nimbostratus and altocumulus.

Cumulus clouds are, in their simplest form, the familiar wool-pack clouds—the soft, fluffy clouds of a spring or summer day. They are caused by currents of warm air rising from heated ground and condensing into visible vapor. If, under different conditions, they spread out and become almost sheet-like, they are called stratocumulus. Sometimes, with the right conditions of heat and moist air, cumulus clouds will begin to build up to great heights and develop into thunderstorms. If rain begins to fall, the clouds are called cumulonimbus.

Fig. 9 Cumulonimbus clouds that have just grown from cumulus. (*U.S. Weather Bureau; F. Ellerman*)

The Weather Bureau official cloud specifications and their code numbers, as used in the international code, are shown in the forecasting section of this book.

You may want to estimate height of the various cloud layers as a part of your observations. These heights may be determined fairly accurately after a little practice, and experienced observers become quite adept at it. The cumulus type cloud is the lowest, usually below 10,000 feet. Clouds with an alto prefix, such as altocumulus and altostratus, are so-called middle clouds, while cirrus clouds are the highest of all, sometimes 30,000 feet or higher. There is no fixed height range for a particular type of cloud, but it is

Fig. 10 Towering cumulus cloud forming over mountains. Shortly after this photograph was taken, rain began falling from dark base of cloud in center of picture.

Fig. 11 Low stratus clouds moving over a small rocky island. (*U.S. Weather Bureau; Ansco*)

well to remember that the *base* of a cloud layer is the elevation given for cloud height.

Sometimes cloud heights are measured by releasing a balloon with known rate of ascent, and timing its ascension until it enters the cloud base. At night a clinometer may be used. The observer, using a spotlight, shines a point of light on the cloud base, then sights this spot through a telescope-like device (the clinometer). Angle of the telescope and distance from the spotlight are used for trigonometric calculation of the cloud height. A fairly new development is the ceilometer, an electronic device for continuous recording of cloud elevation.

18

All of these methods for determining cloud height, however, require a lot of expensive equipment. If you have a Weather Bureau office in or near the town where you live, you might check with it on cloud heights for a while, until you acquire the knack of estimating the height by yourself.

There is, however, an instrument within the price range of many hobbyists' pocketbooks that indicates direction and speed of cloud travel. It is called a nephoscope. A simple one that you may construct will be described later.

Besides type of clouds, their heights, and speed and direction of cloud movement, the weather hobbyist may also wish to note how much of the sky is cloudy. Sky coverage is usually determined in tenths, such as 2/10 cumulus or 7/10 altocumulus.

The hourly Weather Bureau observations, as transmitted on teletype circuits, use the following symbols:

   X *Obscuration (sky completely hidden by precipitation, fog, haze, smoke, etc.)*

  -X *Partial obscuration (1/10 to less than total obscuration)*

  ◯ *Clear (less than 1/10 total sky cover)*

  ⨁ *Scattered clouds (1/10 to less than 6/10 sky cover)*

⊕ *Broken clouds (6/10 to 9/10 sky cover)*

⊕ *Overcast (more than 9/10 sky cover)*

Sometimes the prefixes (−) for a thin and (+) for a dark layer of clouds are used in combination with the scattered, broken or overcast symbols.

Visibility

Visibility is the distance you can see in a horizontal direction, usually expressed in miles and fractions thereof. Sometimes, during rain or fog, visibility may be cut down to a few feet. Select points or landmarks, at known distances from where you live, as visibility markers and use them for determining the distance you can see in various kinds of weather. Visibility over 15 miles is usually considered unlimited and may be so entered on your observation form.

Weather

This is pretty obvious. Here's what we're really looking for. Go as far as you want to in this column. Put down whatever you see from dust devils to hurricanes. The International Weather Code, which is used by the Weather Bureau, recognizes 99 states of weather and combinations thereof—all the way from clear through fog, drizzle, rain and snow to heavy thunderstorm with hail at time of observation. Prefixes like heavy, intermittent, continuous, light and moderate are used. Since you are not coding your observation for international distribution, make your entries any way you care to. If space is limited on your observational form, use symbols, such as S for snow, R for rain, R for thunderstorm, F for fog, et cetera. Use a + for heavy and a − for light. The section on weather map construction gives a complete list of weather symbols.

Put down whatever weather phenomena you see. As you gain experience, you'll find there are things you never noticed before.

Temperature

Get a good thermometer. Enter the temperature in degrees, and tenths if your thermometer has a wide enough scale for this determination.

The best way to expose a thermometer to get true air temperature is to mount it in a slatted or louvered box, called an instrument shelter. This shelter allows free air circulation past the thermometer but protects it from rays of the sun. In the last section of this book are instructions on how to build a shelter. If you don't use a shelter, mount your thermometer on the north

21

side of a building, away from the rays of the sun.

Ordinarily in the United States, air temperature is expressed in degrees Fahrenheit. However, in some upper-air observations, Centigrade temperatures are used.

Formula for converting Centigrade to Fahrenheit:

$$t_f = 9/5 \ t_c \text{ plus } 32°$$

To convert Fahrenheit to Centigrade:

$$t_c = 5/9 \ (t_f \text{ minus } 32°)$$

Dew Point and Relative Humidity

Amount of moisture in the air may be expressed in several ways. The two commonest terms are dew point temperature and relative humidity. You may enter either one on your form—they go hand in hand. Relative humidity is the percentage of water vapor in the air, in relation to the maximum amount of vapor the air can hold at a given temperature without that vapor's changing to visible moisture. Thus, we might say the relative humidity is 75%, meaning that 3/4 as much moisture is present as would be needed for saturation. Dew point is that temperature at which vapor changes to visible moisture, such as fog, dew (from whence the term dew point is taken), et cetera.

The process of changing from visible to invisible moisture is known as evaporation. In this process, water molecules separate and water acquires the properties of a gas. The heat expended in this process is ineffective or latent—that is, it has no power to raise the temperature of the air. Only when vapor is condensed into visible moisture again does heat reappear. Thus evaporation from a moist surface has a cooling effect, because the heat becomes latent or ineffective.

Water vapor, like other gases, exerts a pressure in all directions. This is known as the vapor pressure of the air. As air temperature rises, the amount of water vapor the air can hold increases. Inversely, as the air temperature drops, the amount of water vapor the air can hold decreases. The temperature at which the conversion from invisible to visible moisture is made is the dew point. If the air contains all the vapor it normally can at a given temperature, without the formation of dew or fog, saturation is said to exist. If this saturated air is then cooled, dew or fog will form. The difference between the actual air temperature and the dew point temperature is known as the depression of the dew point.

When moisture condenses, it needs a solid substance upon which the invisible particles can collect and coalesce into visible ones. This explains why moisture will condense on the surface of a glass of ice water.

The cold glass lowers the air temperature near it below the dew point. Invisible moisture thus becomes visible, and the surface of the glass acts as the solid substance upon which this visible moisture can collect.

In the air, dust particles and other microscopic substances form the substance upon which invisible moisture can collect. In this manner fog and clouds are formed. When dust particles, with invisible moisture clinging to them, are carried upward in the air to a layer where the temperature is lower than the dew point, clouds are formed. Fog is formed in the same manner, the only difference being that the process takes place nearer the ground.

One of the instruments used to determine relative humidity or dew point is called a psychrometer. It consists of two thermometers placed side by side, one called the dry bulb thermometer, which shows the air temperature, and the other called the wet bulb thermometer. The bulb of the latter is covered with a layer of wet muslin and indicates the wet bulb temperature. For accurate readings, the two thermometers must be well ventilated. This may be done by mounting them on a sling arrangement and whirling them in a circular motion, or you may have them stationary and ventilate them with a fan. To take a reading, the wet bulb covering, usually a simple muslin cloth, is thoroughly moistened and the thermometers are ven-

Fig. 12 "Pocket" sling psychrometer. (*Courtesy Bendix-Friez*)

tilated. As the wet bulb is cooled by evaporation, the thermometer will show lower and lower readings until it reaches a constant level. The thermometers are then read from time to time, until a constant temperature has been reached. The readings of both wet and dry bulb thermometers are then noted. The amount by which the wet bulb reading is lower than that of the dry bulb is called the wet bulb depression.

With this information, the relative humidity and dew point may now be derived from formulas. As these formulas are rather involved and time-consuming, it is common practice to use prepared tables. Abbreviated tables are shown here. Complete tables may be obtained by writing the Superintendent of Documents, Washington 25, D.C., and asking for Weather Bureau Circular No. 235.

Table showing saturation vapor pressure in inches of mercury and temperature of dew point in degrees Fahrenheit (barometric pressure, 30 inches)

Air Temp. °F.	Saturation Vapor Pressure Inches	Depression of wet bulb thermometer													
		1	2	3	4	6	8	10	12	14	16	18	20	25	30
0	.038	−7	−20												
5	.049	−1	−9	−24											
10	.063	5	−2	−10	−27										
15	.081	11	6	0	−9										
20	.103	16	12	8	2	−21									
25	.130	22	19	15	10	−3	−51								
30	.164	27	25	21	18	8	−7								
35	.203	33	30	28	25	17	7	−11							
40	.247	38	35	33	30	25	18	7	−14						
45	.298	43	41	38	36	31	25	18	7	−14					
50	.360	48	46	44	42	37	32	26	18	8					
55	.432	53	51	50	48	43	38	33	27	20	9	−12			
60	.517	58	57	55	53	49	45	40	35	29	21	11	−8		
65	.616	63	62	60	59	55	51	47	42	37	31	24	14		
70	.732	69	67	65	64	61	57	53	49	44	39	33	26	−11	
75	.866	74	72	71	69	66	63	59	55	51	47	42	36	15	
80	1.022	79	77	76	74	72	68	65	62	58	54	50	44	28	−7
85	1.201	84	82	81	80	77	74	71	68	64	61	57	52	39	19
90	1.408	89	87	86	85	82	79	76	73	70	67	63	59	48	32
95	1.645	94	93	91	90	87	85	82	79	76	73	70	66	56	43
100	1.916	99	98	96	95	93	90	87	85	82	79	76	72	63	52

How to use table: The figures in the left-hand column are the dry bulb, or air temperature, readings. The next column shows the vapor pressure corresponding to these readings.

The figures at the top (1, 2, 3, 4, 6, etc.) are the wet bulb depressions. To find dew point, determine the air temperature and wet bulb depression from reading the psychrometer thermometers, then go across from the air temperature column and find the figure in the vertical column that falls under the proper wet bulb depression figure. For example: Air temperature, 70°, wet bulb depression, 10. The dew point is then found to be 53. For temperatures and wet bulb depressions falling between the figures given, you will have to interpolate. Regular Weather Bureau tables are more complete and little or no interpolation is necessary.

Table showing relative humidity, percent, using Fahrenheit temperatures (barometric pressure, 30 inches)

Air Temp. °F.	Depression of wet bulb thermometer													
	1	2	3	4	6	8	10	12	14	16	18	20	25	30
0	67	33												
5	73	46	20											
10	78	56	34	13										
15	82	64	46	29										
20	85	70	55	40	12									
25	87	74	62	49	25	1								
30	89	78	67	56	36	16								
35	91	81	72	63	45	27	10							
40	92	83	75	68	52	37	22	7						
45	93	86	78	71	57	44	31	18	6					
50	93	87	80	74	61	49	38	27	16	5				
55	94	88	82	76	65	54	43	33	23	14	5			
60	94	89	83	78	68	58	48	39	30	21	13	5		
65	95	90	85	80	70	61	52	44	35	27	20	12		
70	95	90	86	81	72	64	55	48	40	33	25	19	3	
75	96	91	86	82	74	66	58	51	44	37	30	24	9	
80	96	91	87	83	75	68	61	54	47	41	35	29	15	3
85	96	92	88	84	76	70	62	56	50	44	38	32	20	8
90	96	92	89	85	78	71	65	58	52	47	41	36	24	10
95	96	93	89	86	79	72	66	60	54	50	44	38	28	17
100	96	93	89	86	80	73	68	62	56	51	46	41	30	21

How to use table: The figures in the left-hand column are the dry bulb, or air temperature, readings.

The figures at the top (1, 2, 3, 4, 6, etc.) are the wet bulb depressions. To find relative humidity, determine the air temperature and wet bulb depression from reading the psychrometer thermometers, then go across from the air temperature column and find the figure in the vertical column that falls under the proper wet bulb depression figure. For example: Air temperature, 70°, wet bulb depression, 10. The relative humidity is then found to be 55%.

Fig. 13 Hygro-thermograph. This instrument records temperature and relative humidity. (*Courtesy Bendix-Friez*)

A second instrument used to determine relative humidity is the hair hygrometer. It has been found that human hair, if properly cleaned and treated, will lengthen as the relative humidity increases. This principle is used in the construction of the hair hygrometer. Through a system of linkage, a strand or group of strands of human hair is connected to an indicating pointer. As these strands are lengthened or shortened by variations in relative humidity, the pointer fluctuates and relative humidity is shown on a calibrated scale. A recording hygrometer or hygrograph works on the same principle, the only difference being that the pointer is an arm and pen that records relative humidity on a moving paper chart. The hair hygrometer is not as accurate as the psychrometer described above and must, in fact, be frequently corrected by comparison to the wet and dry bulb instrument.

Actually, relative humidity and dew point may not be too important to you if your interest in weather is mostly a matter of keeping a daily record. If such is the case you may want to omit them from your form. But if you get into forecasting, they will become more important. We will go further into the subject in the forecasting section of this book.

Wind Direction and Velocity

Wind direction is easy to determine. Any method from watching chimney smoke to maintaining one of the devices for continuously recording wind direction and velocity may be used. Generally speaking, wind is said to be in one of the eight compass directions—North, Northeast, East, et cetera, although it sometimes is recorded to 16 points—North, North-northeast, Northeast, East-northeast. . . . Actual compass degrees may also be used, as 90 degrees for an east wind, 180 degrees for a south wind, 270 degrees for a west wind and 360 degrees for a north

29

Fig. 14 Wind vane and anemometer. These instruments transmit wind direction and velocity to the indicator shown in Figure 15, or the recorder shown in Figure 16. (*Courtesy The Instruments Corporation*)

wind. Remember that wind direction is that direction *from which* the wind is blowing. Suggestions for building a wind vane are included in the final section of this book.

Wind velocity is usually expressed in miles-per-hour. It is most accurately determined by an anemometer. A familiar type is the rotating cup or cone type, seen at airports and on government buildings. The cups on such an anemometer are rotated by the wind, and the rotations are then converted into miles-per-

Fig. 15   Wind direction and velocity indicating dials.
(*Courtesy The Instruments Corporation*)

Fig. 16   Wind direction and velocity recorder. (*Courtesy The Instruments Corporation*)

hour by a mechanical or electrical system. The final section of this book also contains directions for making your own anemometer.

31

A number of years ago, a British admiral by the name of Sir Francis Beaufort worked out a fairly accurate system for determining wind speeds. This wind scale is as follows:

Beaufort No.	Miles per hour on land	Type of wind	Identifying signs
0	Less than 1	Calm	Smoke rises in vertical columns
1	1 - 3	Light air	Smoke drifts, wind vanes do not respond
2	4 - 7	Light breeze	Leaves rustle; wind can be felt on face
3	8-12	Gentle breeze	Light flags extended; leaves, small twigs move constantly
4	13-18	Moderate breeze	Dust, loose paper blown about; small branches move
5	19-24	Fresh breeze	Small trees in leaf start to sway; crested wavelets visible on inland waters
6	25-31	Strong breeze	Large branches moving; telegraph wires whistle; umbrellas hard to use
7	32-38	Moderate gale	Whole trees in motion; difficult to walk against wind
8	39-46	Fresh gale	Twigs broken from trees; affects moving vehicles
9	47-54	Strong gale	Slight damage to buildings—slates, chimney pots, etc., blown off
10	55-63	Whole gale	Rarely experienced inland; considerable building damage; trees uprooted
11	64-75	Storm	Very rare; causes widespread damage
12	Above 75	Hurricane	Extremely destructive to everything in its path

The Weather Bureau terms for various Beaufort numbers are: 0, 1, 2—light wind; 3—gentle; 4—moderate; 5—fresh; 6, 7—strong; 8, 9—gale; 10, 11—whole gale; 12—hurricane.

Fig. 17 Microbarograph for recording atmospheric pressure. (*Courtesy Bendix-Friez*)

Barometric Pressure

We live at the bottom of a sea of gases which we call the atmosphere. The main components of this gaseous sea (we know it more familiarly as air) are oxygen (21%), nitrogen (78%) and miscellaneous gases, such as argon, neon, etc., (the remaining 1%).

The atmosphere has weight. To determine this weight is the function of the barometer. Another way

33

of explaining its function is to say the barometer measures the downward pressure of the air at a particular point.

The most accurate instrument for determining barometric pressure is the mercurial barometer. This instrument balances weight of the atmosphere against weight of a column of mercury in a glass tube. Another (and usually cheaper) barometer is the aneroid barometer. In it, the pressure exerts a force on an elastic diaphragm and, through a linkage system, this pressure is indicated on a dial. While some aneroid barometers are not very accurate, there are good ones available. In addition to indicating barometers, there are recording barometers or barographs, which make a continuous record of atmospheric pressure.

Barometric pressure is sometimes expressed in inches of mercury, although millibars are used by most professional weather services. One inch equals 33.86395 millibars. Usually aneroid barometers use the inch scale. Here is a chart for converting inches into millibars.

Table for converting barometric inches (mercury) into millibars

In.	.00 mb.	.01 mb.	.02 mb.	.03 mb.	.04 mb.	.05 mb.	.06 mb.	.07 mb.	.08 mb.	.09 mb.
27.5	931.3	931.6	931.9	932.3	932.6	933.0	933.3	933.6	934.0	934.3
27.6	934.6	935.0	935.3	935.7	936.0	936.3	936.7	937.0	937.4	937.7
27.7	938.0	938.4	938.7	939.0	939.4	939.7	940.1	940.4	940.7	941.1
27.8	941.4	941.8	942.1	942.4	942.8	943.1	943.4	943.8	944.1	944.5
27.9	944.8	945.1	945.5	945.8	946.2	946.5	946.8	947.2	947.5	947.9
28.0	948.2	948.5	948.9	949.2	949.5	949.9	950.2	950.6	950.9	951.2
28.1	951.6	951.9	952.3	952.6	952.9	953.3	953.6	953.9	954.3	954.6
28.2	955.0	955.3	955.6	956.0	956.3	956.7	957.0	957.3	957.7	958.0
28.3	958.3	958.7	959.0	959.4	959.7	960.0	960.4	960.7	961.1	961.4
28.4	961.7	962.1	962.4	962.8	963.1	963.4	963.8	964.1	964.4	964.8
28.5	965.1	965.5	965.8	966.1	966.5	966.8	967.2	967.5	967.8	968.2
28.6	968.5	968.8	969.2	969.5	969.9	970.2	970.5	970.9	971.2	971.6
28.7	971.9	972.2	972.6	972.9	973.2	973.6	973.9	974.3	974.6	974.9
28.8	975.3	975.6	976.0	976.3	976.6	977.0	977.3	977.7	978.0	978.3
28.9	978.7	979.0	979.3	979.7	980.0	980.4	980.7	981.0	981.4	981.7
29.0	982.1	982.4	982.7	983.1	983.4	983.7	984.1	984.4	984.8	985.1
29.1	985.4	985.8	986.1	986.5	986.8	987.1	987.5	987.8	988.2	988.5
29.2	988.8	989.2	989.5	989.8	990.2	990.5	990.9	991.2	991.5	991.9
29.3	992.2	992.6	992.9	993.2	993.6	993.9	994.2	994.6	994.9	995.3
29.4	995.6	995.9	996.3	996.6	997.0	997.3	997.6	998.0	998.3	998.6
29.5	999.0	999.3	999.7	1000.0	1000.3	1000.7	1001.0	1001.4	1001.7	1002.0
29.6	1002.4	1002.7	1003.1	1003.4	1003.7	1004.1	1004.4	1004.7	1005.1	1005.4
29.7	1005.8	1006.1	1006.4	1006.8	1007.1	1007.5	1007.8	1008.1	1008.5	1008.8

Table for converting barometric inches (mercury) into millibars (continued)

In.	.00 mb.	.01 mb.	.02 mb.	.03 mb.	.04 mb.	.05 mb.	.06 mb.	.07 mb.	.08 mb.	.09 mb.
29.8	1009.1	1009.5	1009.8	1010.2	1010.5	1010.8	1011.2	1011.5	1011.9	1012.2
29.9	1012.5	1012.9	1013.2	1013.5	1013.9	1014.2	1014.6	1014.9	1015.2	1015.6
30.0	1015.9	1016.3	1016.6	1016.9	1017.3	1017.6	1018.0	1018.3	1018.6	1019.0
30.1	1019.3	1019.6	1020.0	1020.3	1020.7	1021.0	1021.3	1021.7	1022.0	1022.4
30.2	1022.7	1023.0	1023.4	1023.7	1024.0	1024.4	1024.7	1025.1	1025.4	1025.7
30.3	1026.1	1026.4	1026.8	1027.1	1027.4	1027.8	1028.1	1028.4	1028.8	1029.1
30.4	1029.5	1029.8	1030.1	1030.5	1030.8	1031.2	1031.5	1031.8	1032.2	1032.5
30.5	1032.9	1033.2	1033.5	1033.9	1034.2	1034.5	1034.9	1035.2	1035.6	1035.9
30.6	1036.2	1036.6	1036.9	1037.3	1037.6	1037.9	1038.3	1038.6	1038.9	1039.3
30.7	1039.6	1040.0	1040.3	1040.6	1041.0	1041.3	1041.7	1042.0	1042.3	1042.7
30.8	1043.0	1043.3	1043.7	1044.0	1044.4	1044.7	1045.0	1045.4	1045.7	1046.1
30.9	1046.4	1046.7	1047.1	1047.4	1047.8	1048.1	1048.4	1048.8	1049.1	1049.5
31.0	1049.8	1050.1	1050.5	1050.8	1051.1	1051.5	1051.8	1052.2	1052.5	1052.8
31.1	1053.2	1053.5	1053.8	1054.2	1054.5	1054.9	1055.2	1055.5	1055.9	1056.2
31.2	1056.6	1056.9	1057.2	1057.6	1057.9	1058.2	1058.6	1058.9	1059.3	1059.6
31.3	1059.9	1060.3	1060.6	1061.0	1061.3	1061.6	1062.0	1062.3	1062.7	1063.0
31.4	1063.3	1063.7	1064.0	1064.3	1064.7	1065.0	1065.4	1065.7	1066.0	1066.4
31.5	1066.7	1067.1	1067.4	1067.7	1068.1	1068.4	1068.7	1069.1	1069.4	1069.8
31.6	1070.1	1070.4	1070.8	1071.1	1071.5	1071.8	1072.1	1072.5	1072.8	1073.1
31.7	1073.5	1073.8	1074.2	1074.5	1074.8	1075.2	1075.5	1075.9	1076.2	1076.5
31.8	1076.9	1077.2	1077.6	1077.9	1078.2	1078.6	1078.9	1079.2	1079.6	1079.9
31.9	1080.3	1080.6	1080.9	1081.3	1081.6	1082.0	1082.3	1082.6	1083.0	1083.3

Later in this book we will discuss high and low pressure areas and how their movement across the country affects the weather. If your interest in meteorology includes forecasting, measuring the changes in pressure as these highs and lows move across your area is an important part of your observation.

Forecasting interests itself mainly in the *changing* of barometric pressure. And the words Rain, Change, Fair, and so forth, printed on the dial of a barometer do not mean much and should not be considered seriously by the amateur meteorologist.

You may use either station or sea-level pressure on your observation form. Station pressure is the actual pressure at the place of observation. Since air has weight, the pressure at sea level will naturally be greater than on a mountain top. In the interests of standardization, whenever a barometer reading is transmitted over nationwide circuits, it is converted to sea-level pressure. This is done to facilitate the drawing of weather maps.

A mercurial barometer reads directly in station pressure after corrections for temperature have been made. If you buy an aneroid barometer, directions for setting will come with it.

Amount of Rain or Snow

Rain is generally measured in hundredths of an

inch, and to get an accurate measurement a rain gage is used. While any straight-sided vessel may be used, to get a more accurate measurement it is advisable to have a gage built so that water can be measured in multiples of the rain that has actually fallen.

Most rain gages use a funnel arrangement. The rain is funneled into a tube which has a cross-sectional area equal to a fraction (usually 1/10) of that of the funnel. If 1/10 is used, 0.01 in. of rain will measure 0.1 in. in the tube, which amount can be accurately measured with a ruler.

For snowfall, a simple, straight-sided vessel will do, or you may measure the snowfall at several points on the ground. Remember that precipitation should be measured as soon as possible after it falls so that evaporation will not lessen the reading. Gages are available commercially that make a continuous record of precipitation. In the last section of this book are instructions for building a simple rain gage.

Maximum and Minimum Temperature Since Last Observation

The highest and lowest temperatures in a given period are indicated on special thermometers called maximum and minimum thermometers. The maximum thermometer is similar to the common clinical thermometer. As the mercury flows out of the bulb and into the stem, it passes through a constriction in the column (or bore). When the temperature rises, mercury is forced upward through this constriction. But when the temperature starts to drop, the mercury column, instead of receding back into the bulb, "breaks" at the constriction. The top end of the mercury column thus remains at that point on the scale reached by the highest temperature. To reset the maximum thermometer, it is whirled on its special mounting and this motion forces the mercury back in the bulb.

The minimum thermometer uses alcohol, instead of mercury, as its fluid. A minute dumbbell-shaped "index" floats in the alcohol column. As the temperature falls, surface tension at the top of the alcohol column carries the index down the temperature scale. When the minimum temperature is reached, and the alcohol column starts to rise, the index stays at its lowest position, registering the lowest temperature. Maximum and minimum thermometers are usually clamped on the same, special mounting. They are both normally placed in an almost horizontal position, with the maximum thermometer on a bearing so it may be rapidly rotated for resetting. To reset the minimum thermometer, its bulb end is raised so the index will return to the top of the alcohol column.

39

There are other instruments for registering maximum and minimum temperatures. One is a dial-type, bimetallic thermometer that has two pointer-like indexes. One index is pushed toward the high end of the thermometer scale as the regular thermometer pointer rises, while the other is pushed toward the low end as the temperature drops. Some of this type are fairly accurate, although not as reliable as the mercury and alcohol types described above.

Still another type uses both mercury and alcohol in one column. It has indexes for both maximum and minimum temperatures which ride in the column, similar to the principle of the minimum thermometer described above. These indexes are of a magnetic material and are reset with a small magnet. Good accuracy is obtained in some instruments of this type.

A continuously recording thermometer, called a thermograph, is used at some stations. By means of a rotating, clock-driven chart, the thermograph makes a complete record of all temperature variations, either for a 24-hour period or for a week. Usually the latter is preferred.

Remarks

You may enter any pertinent data on the weather in this column—possibly weather that may have occurred since your last regular observation, etc. This is a pretty obvious place to put down what you didn't enter somewhere else on the form.

How the Professional Services Handle Observations

The Weather Bureau makes four primary weather observations in each 24-hour period at its stations in the United States. These observations are made at 1:30 and 7:30 A.M. and 1:30 and 7:30 P.M., Eastern Standard Time. Observations must be made simultaneously at all stations across the country so that weather maps and charts may be drawn for a definite time of day. Thus when a Weather Bureau observer is making an observation at 7:30 in the evening in New York, another observer in San Francisco is taking his readings at the same moment, although it is only 4:30 P.M. out there. Weather stations all over the world observe these same times for taking their weather data. Greenwich Civil Time is used as a reference for worldwide weather observations.

In addition to these main observations, four intermediate observations are made at many stations. These fall midway between the regular observation times shown above.

When the observations are completed, they are put into a code form and transmitted nationally and inter-

41

Fig. 18 Exposure of instruments, Central Office Observatory, Washington, D.C. (*U.S. Weather Bureau*)

nationally by teletype and radio. In the United States and Canada, the principal methods of distributing coded reports (synoptic reports) is by teletype, although telegraph, radio and telephone are sometimes used when teletype circuits are not available. Coded reports are exchanged on a worldwide basis by radio. In the next section of this book, methods used in the coding and decoding of weather observations will be discussed.

Observing

In addition to these standard observations used for drawing the six-hourly, and sometimes three-hourly, weather maps, many weather stations in the United States, Alaska and Canada take regular hourly observations, mainly for use in aviation. Some stations also take an auxiliary half-hourly observation. These observations are briefer than the regular six-hourly observations and are put on regional and national teletype circuits each hour. If significant weather changes occur between observations, a special weather observation is also made and put on the teletype circuits. An observer at a regular airways weather station must be constantly on the lookout for development of thunderstorms, fog conditions, wind shifts, etc., so that a special observation may be made and distributed to all concerned.

In addition to being distributed by teletype, the hourly observations are broadcast over Civil Aeronautics Authority radio range stations and other radio facilities.

3

Forecasting

The ultimate goal of the serious meteorologist is to forecast the weather accurately. As you gain experience in observing the weather, you will, more or less unconsciously, absorb much information valuable in forecasting. There is no simple formula, no calibrated mechanism that makes weather predicting a snap. Rather, forecasting is a skill requiring long study and patience. As we shall see later, an important aid to the forecaster is a continuing picture of the movement across the country of high- and low-pressure systems and their associated air masses and fronts. This is

44

graphically represented on surface weather maps. In addition, the serious forecaster has charts of upper air conditions, winds aloft and temperature and moisture conditions as determined by instruments carried aloft by balloons and airplanes.

The amateur forecaster can become quite adept at forecasting for his immediate vicinity by keeping track of the conditions that precede the different kinds of weather. Then, when a similar set of conditions occurs, he will know what to expect.

On the following pages, we will give suggestions to help you get started on forecasting for your immediate area. Later we will discuss how to use weather maps and other aids for more accurate forecasting. Since forecasting is a vast subject and many textbooks are available, the information given here will deal mainly with ways of collecting and interpreting data, map drawing, et cetera.

Forecasting from Local Conditions

The study of the relationship between plant and animal life and the weather is called phenology. By observing such phenomena as thickness of fur on certain animals, markings on the backs of caterpillars or the flowering of certain plants, some supporters of this science claim they can predict the weather. Actually, changes such as those listed above do not occur until the weather causing them has already taken place.

People who work outdoors a lot, however, often become good at forecasting the weather, simply by watching it from day to day and dipping into their memory for conditions of a like nature that have produced certain types of weather in the past.

Clouds—kind, how fast they are traveling and in what direction—are one of the best indications of future weather conditions. Here are some generalized rules for predicting weather by observing the clouds.

Cirrus clouds, as described in the observing section of this book, are the high fibrous, wispy types, usually with indefinite edges. They are often beautifully colored at sunrise and sunset. Composed of ice crystals, these clouds have bases usually above 20,000 feet. If cirrus clouds are not thickening, they generally indicate fair weather ahead. However, if they seem to thicken and are followed by lower clouds, rain or snow usually follows in 12 to 24 hours. The thickening and lowering indicates that a warm front is moving in, preceding a mass of warmer, moisture-laden air.

When cirrocumulus clouds (patches of small, white puffs) appear, the sky is sometimes referred to as a mackerel sky. Cirrocumulus is always accompanied by some other type of cirrus cloud. This latter type of cloud, composed of ice crystals, may indicate rain and

46

warmer temperatures if followed by lower and thicker clouds.

Cirrostratus are the thin, sheet-like clouds that sometimes cover the entire sky. They are composed of ice crystals. A large circle or halo can be observed when they pass in front of the sun or moon. This halo produces a rainbow effect, with blue on the outside and red on the inside of the ring. If cirrostratus clouds seem to be breaking up into cirrocumulus, fair weather lies ahead. But if the sheet-like appearance persists, chances are good for rain and warmer readings. Cirrostratus clouds are usually associated with a warm front.

Altocumulus and altostratus clouds are so-called middle clouds. Their bases can be anywhere between 6,500 and 20,000 feet above the earth. Altocumulus are usually composed of water droplets. They appear as small, isolated patches or parallel bands. Generally speaking, the shape and altitude of altocumulus clouds are continually changing. When they pass in front of the sun or moon, a small rainbow-like ring or corona appears, red on the outside and blue inside. Occasionally also may be seen wispy trails of precipitation, called virga, extending from them. Virga is precipitation that evaporates before it reaches the ground. If altocumulus clouds are thick enough, light rain or snow may fall to the ground. This type of cloud often

47

precedes a front and may merge into rain-bearing altostratus.

Altostratus clouds are the veil or sheet-like type with a gray or blue appearance. The sun or moon becomes a diffused spot when clouds of this kind pass in front of them. Altostratus clouds usually consist of water droplets, although the upper portion may be composed of ice crystals. Steady rain or snow can fall from altostratus clouds. They may precede either a cold or warm front and, when they appear to be darkening, indicate stormy weather.

Low clouds have their bases close to the ground while their average upper level is only 6,500 feet. Stratocumulus clouds fall within this range. They occur as a continuous sheet or as patches or rolls with a wave-like appearance. Sometimes formed by the flattening and spreading out of cumulus clouds, they are composed of water droplets and may be accompanied by light drizzle or snow showers. Stratocumulus clouds often form in the vicinity of thunderstorms and along warm and cold fronts. From a forecasting standpoint, they indicate a change in the weather.

Stratus clouds are uniform layers of indefinite shape, resembling fog. As a matter of fact, if they rest on the ground they are called fog. Often stratus clouds are very thin and cause a hazy appearance in the sky. Light drizzle or snow flurries may accompany the

48

presence of a layer of stratus. Fair weather may follow stratus and the sun will usually clear up (burn off) a nighttime layer of these clouds.

When stratus clouds form in thick layers, they are called nimbostratus. This type is accompanied by steady rain or snow. Nimbostratus clouds are dark gray in color and their bases are ragged and indefinite in outline. These clouds precede periods of warm frontal conditions and may bring long, steady rain.

The lowest clouds are of the cumulus type, and their bases are on the average only 1,600 feet above ground. However, under the right conditions of moisture and rising currents of warm air, they may build up to great heights—sometimes even to the high, cirrus level. The ordinary fair-weather cumulus seen on spring and summer days have the appearance of cotton tufts or wool packs. They never overcast the sky, and often turn into stratocumulus or altocumulus in late afternoon, to disappear at night. Fair weather cumulus usually form in the cool air following a cold front and indicate a period of nice weather ahead.

But not all the cumulus of a warm summer day promise fair skies. Those which seem to swell and boil upward may be forerunners of thunderstorms, especially if they form early on summer mornings. They sometimes precede a warm front and indicate a change to warmer weather conditions.

49

Cumulonimbus clouds are massive, cauliflower-shaped clouds whose tops have reached or gone above the freezing level into the cirrus cloud region. Their bases are dark and ragged, and rain—sometimes heavy—accompanies them. These are the clouds of thunderstorms, sometimes severe, with hail and even tornado development if conditions are right. Towering cumulonimbus sometimes form along lines, called squall lines, ahead of cold fronts, and make a very impressive sight as they approach from the west or southwest. With the approach of these cumulonimbus (thunderheads), you can expect rain, thunder and lightning.

Clouds tell the weather observer and forecaster many things. While there are no strict rules for predicting weather by watching clouds, skill may be acquired by studying clouds and observing the weather that follows. After a period of cloud and weather study, you will be able to "read" clouds and predict weather with some degree of accuracy for your particular locality.

Wind and barometer indications also offer a clue to future weather conditions and should be studied by the amateur meteorologist interested in weather forecasting. Although a particular reading of the barometer does not mean much in itself, the amount of rise or fall in pressure and the rate of this change may give important clues to future weather. As a rule, winds from the east quadrants and a falling barometer indicate stormy weather, while winds shifting to the west quadrants indicate clearing and fair weather. There are certain wind-barometer indications that are generally applicable to all parts of the country, and the Weather Bureau furnishes the following general rules for wind-barometer indications.

When the wind sets in from points between south and southeast and the barometer falls steadily, a storm is approaching from the west or northwest, and its center will pass near or north of the observer within 12 to 24 hours, with winds shifting to northwest by way of south and southwest.

When the wind sets in from points between east and northeast, and the barometer falls steadily, a storm is approaching from the south or southwest, and its center will pass near or to the south of the observer within 12 to 24 hours, with winds shifting to northwest by way of north. The rapidity of the storm's approach and its intensity will be indicated by the rate and amount of fall in the barometer.

The Weather Bureau has also prepared a more detailed table on wind and barometer indications on the following page:

51

FORECASTING

Table of Wind and Barometer Indications

Wind Direction	Barometer Reading Reduced to Sea Level	Weather Forecast
SW to NW	30.10 to 30.20 and steady	Fair, with slight temperature changes, for 1 to 2 days
SW to NW	30.10 to 30.20 and rising rapidly	Fair, followed within 2 days by rain
SW to NW	30.20 and above, and stationary	Continued fair, with no decided temperature change
SW to NW	30.20 and above and falling slowly	Slowly rising temperature and fair for 2 days
S to SE	30.10 to 30.20 and falling slowly	Rain within 24 hours
S to SE	30.10 to 30.20 and falling rapidly	Wind increasing in force, with rain within 12 to 24 hours
SE to NE	30.10 to 30.20 and falling slowly	Rain in 12 to 18 hours
SE to NE	30.10 to 30.20 and falling rapidly	Increasing wind, and rain within 12 hours
E to NE	30.10 and above and falling slowly	In summer, with light winds, rain may not fall for several days. In winter, rain within 24 hours
E to NE	30.10 and above and falling rapidly	In summer, rain probable within 12 to 24 hours. In winter, rain or snow, with increasing winds, often will set in when barometer begins to fall and the wind sets in from the NE
SE to NE	30.00 or below and falling slowly	Rain will continue 1 to 2 days
SE to NE	30.00 or below and falling rapidly	Rain, with high wind, followed within 36 hours by clearing, and in winter by colder
S to SW	30.00 or below and rising slowly	Clearing within a few hours, and fair for several days
S to E	29.80 or below and falling rapidly	Severe storm imminent, followed within 24 hours by clearing, and in winter by colder
E to N	29.80 or below and falling rapidly	Severe northeast gale and heavy precipitation; in winter, heavy snow followed by a cold wave
Going to W	29.80 or below and rising rapidly	Clearing and colder

52

There are many weather sayings, some with a scientific basis and others with no basis in truth at all. Thus memorizing various clichés seems out of place here.

The best way to become good with your forecasting is to note conditions and effects in your own area. A forecasting rule that may apply in California may mean nothing in Virginia. Here are some general rules for predicting weather changes. But they may need to be altered for your particular geographical location.

Look for a change to stormy conditions when:

> *The barometer shows a steady fall.*

> *Clouds get thicker and darker.*

> *Lower clouds move in from a southerly or easterly direction and travel with good speed.*

> *The wind shifts to the south or east.*

> *The temperature shows an abrupt rise, there is a flow of moist air from the south, and fog may form.*

> *After a day or two of westerly or northerly winds, the wind velocity drops at sunset and the sun sets clear or with a few cirrus clouds in the west.*

> *You suspect the approach of a warm or cold front.*

FORECASTING

Look for a change to fair weather when:

> *The barometer rises rapidly.*

> *Clouds appear to break up and clear patches of sky show.*

> *The wind shifts to a westerly or northwesterly direction, indicating passage of a cold front.*

> *Bases of clouds increase in elevation.*

Look for continuing fair weather when:

> *The barometer remains steady or rises.*

> *Temperature is normal.*

> *Stratus clouds or fog dissipate in the morning.*

> *The wind continues to blow from a westerly direction.*

> *The sun sets clear.*

> *There is dew or frost at night.*

Look for colder weather when:

> *The wind shifts to the west or northwest.*

> *A cold front has passed.*

> *A westerly wind drops in velocity at night and the sun sets clear.*

The pressure rises.

Clouds break up after a storm and the northern sky seems to have a greenish tinge (in winter).

Look for warmer weather when:

It is cloudy at night.

A northwest wind has become calm and later begins to blow from the south.

A warm front has passed.

Weather Maps

The surface weather map, along with charts of winds aloft and upper air temperature and moisture conditions, furnishes real working material for the forecaster. Weather maps appearing in some newspapers are a familiar feature and prove a big help in making forecasts, either for a particular location or a wide area. Some newspaper maps are so simplified, however, that they leave out important data and thus are of little use. This applies particularly to the syndicated maps distributed to various newspapers across the country. But some newspaper maps are drawn up by Weather Bureau personnel and furnished to papers in the town or city where the Weather Bureau office

55

is located. These maps are quite complete and detailed and prove very beneficial in forecasting.

By far the best map available for public distribution is the daily printed weather map produced in Washington, D.C., by the Weather Bureau and obtainable from the Superintendent of Documents on a subscription basis. This map shows the 1:30 A.M. surface weather for the United States, the barometric and frontal pattern over North America as it existed 12 hours previously, precipitation totals for a 24-hour period, highest and lowest temperatures for the previous 24 hours, and the 700-millibar constant pressure chart. The subscription price is sixty cents a month.

Data for regular weather maps is collected at six-hourly intervals, as explained in the section on observing. This data is put into code form, in accordance with international agreement, and distributed to weather offices in this country and to most countries of the world. As each weather station receives the reports, they are decoded and entries are made on base maps. So-called manuscript maps are then drawn up, showing, for instance, lines of equal barometric pressure (isobars), clouds and temperatures.

In the United States, six-hourly map data is broadcast by Short Wave Stations WEK, New Orleans, Louisiana, and WSY, New York City. These broadcasts are in International Morse Code. In addition, beginning on the hour during each period of broadcast, Station WEK broadcasts a radio teletype signal for a 15-minute period. This teletype broadcast uses frequency-shift keying. If the amateur meteorologist is able to build receiving and conversion circuits, he can receive teletype weather messages in his own home. This might be a fairly simple procedure for the weather hobbyist who is also a radio amateur. Information on setting up radio teletype equipment is available in such amateur radio magazines as *QST* and *CQ*. There are used teletype machines on the market and the only other equipment needed for teletype reception is a good short-wave receiver and a frequency-shift converter which can be built with regular radio parts. The amateur interested in radio teletype reception of weather map data is advised to contact the magazines mentioned above for data and copies of back issues dealing with construction of such equipment.

To receive the broadcasts in International Morse Code, you will need a short-wave receiver and ability to copy the code. It is possible to build a code printer that will print code directly on paper tape. Information on construction of this equipment is likewise available from the magazines listed above. Code printers can also be bought ready-made. Since construction of electronic code and teletype printing equipment requires a knowledge of radio, we will not go into it in this book. There are many good textbooks available covering the subject.

International Morse Code

A · —		S · · ·	
B — · · ·		T —	
C — · — ·		U · · —	
D — · ·		V · · · —	
E ·		W · — —	
F · · — ·		X — · · —	
G — — ·		Y — · — —	
H · · · ·		Z — — · ·	
I · ·		1 · — — — —	
J · — — —		2 · · — — —	
K — · —		3 · · · — —	
L · — · ·		4 · · · · —	
M — —		5 · · · · ·	
N — ·		6 — · · · ·	
O — — —		7 — — · · ·	
P · — — ·		8 — — — · ·	
Q — — · —		9 — — — — ·	
R · — ·		0 — — — — —	
		(or ———)	

Punctuation and Special Signals

Period (.) · — · — · —   = — · · · —

Comma (,) — — · · — —   / — · · — ·

From (de) — · · ·   ? · · — — · ·

Go Ahead (k) — · —

Understood (VE) · · · — ·

End of Message (cross x) · — · — ·

Transmission Finished (sk) · · · — · —

The broadcasts from Stations WSY and WEK are

sent at a speed corresponding to about 20 words per minute. WSY operates on frequencies of 5947.5, 8125, 13620 and 16250 kilocycles. WEK operates on frequencies of 4062.5, 8140, 13624 and 18765 kilocycles.

In addition to coded reports giving data for surface weather maps, upper air, ship and storm advisories and analyses of surface conditions are also broadcast. Since times for these various broadcast parts vary somewhat, it is advisable to spend some time copying reports from these stations to determine times when the various information is sent. At the beginning of each transmission, information to be broadcast is listed in plain language, not code. Thus a broadcast might start with such identifying information as Analyses or Ship or Synop (synoptic weather map observations). However, this is the only part of the broadcast using plain English. Because so much information is packed into these broadcasts, if each item were named and described in plain language, a long message would be required. This would be confusing to read and difficult to transfer to a map. Persons trained in the use of the code can read the message as easily as plain language.

There are, then, three ways of getting together weather maps—by buying them already drawn from the Superintendent of Documents, Washington 25, D.C.; by depending on the one appearing in your daily newspaper; or by drawing your own from information

59

obtained by the methods described above. Obviously, the last-named, while the most difficult, furnishes the most timely information.

If you decide to draw your own weather map, you will need a supply of base maps for plotting the decoded weather information. One type of map is available from the Superintendent of Documents. Or it may be possible to buy base maps at some stationery stores.

A good method is to draw up a base map of your own and reproduce copies of it by the hectograph method described in the observing section of this book (pp. 8-9), or by one of the other reproduction methods mentioned. Some road maps of the United States, available at filling stations, are of a convenient size to guide you in drawing your base map. It is a good idea, however, to get a look at the maps used in Weather Bureau offices as a model for the one you decide on.

If you draw up your own base maps but do not want to make up a big supply, a good method is to transfer a map to a sheet of drawing paper by the carbon paper method. Or if you do not care to preserve back copies of your maps, there is still another method you might use. Draw up a base map on a good grade of drawing paper, using black drawing ink. Cover this map with a sheet of glass (you may want to use an old picture frame with glass for mounting it) and do your plotting with grease or china-marking pencils. When you are ready to re-plot the map with new observations, simply rub out the old entries with a dry rag and go ahead with the new plotting.

The base maps supplied by the Superintendent of Documents show only the names of cities in which Weather Bureau stations are located. They do not give the station numbers or show the station circle. They are, in fact, the base maps upon which the daily subscription weather map data is over-printed.

Weather Bureau stations in the United States and Canada are designated by both a number and letters. Numbers are used in transmission of the international weather code and the letters are used for the hourly observations directed mainly toward aviation needs.

Some of the station numbers and letters are listed below. If you are interested in a more complete listing of the stations in your area, you may obtain it at a Weather Bureau office near you.

202	MIA	Miami, Fla.	248	SHV	Shreveport, La.
206	JAX	Jacksonville, Fla.	250	BRO	Brownsville, Tex.
208	CHS	Charleston, S.C.	266	ABI	Abilene, Tex.
214	TLH	Tallahassee, Fla.	270	ELP	El Paso, Tex.
219	ATL	Atlanta, Ga.	274	TUS	Tucson, Ariz.
228	BHM	Birmingham, Ala.	290-SAN		San Diego, Calif.
235	JAN	Jackson, Miss.	304	HAT	Cape Hatteras,
242	GLS	Galveston, Tex.			N.C.

61

306 RDU	Raleigh, N.C.	534 CHI	Chicago, Ill.
327 BNA	Nashville, Tenn.	546 DSM	Des Moines, Iowa
340 LIT	Little Rock, Ark.	553 OMA	Omaha, Nebr.
363 AMA	Amarillo, Tex.	562 LBF	North Platte,
365 ABQ	Albuquerque,		Nebr.
	N.M.	564 CYS	Cheyenne, Wyo.
374 INW	Winslow, Ariz.	569 CPR	Casper, Wyo.
386 LSV	Las Vegas, Nev.	572 SLC	Salt Lake City,
— 389 FAT	Fresno, Calif.		Utah
405 DCA	Washington, D.C.	583 WMC	Winnemucca,
413 PKV	Pikeville, Ky.		Nev.
417 EKN	Elkins, W. Va.	594 EUR	Eureka, Calif.
423 SDF	Louisville, Ky.	639 APN	Alpena, Mich.
428 CMH	Columbus, Ohio	641 MSN	Madison, Wis.
434 STL	St. Louis, Mo.	648 ESC	Escanaba, Mich.
438 IND	Indianapolis, Ind.	654 HON	Huron, S.D.
440 SGF	Springfield, Mo.	658 MSP	Minneapolis,
446 MKC	Kansas City, Mo.		Minn.
451 DDC	Dodge City, Kan.	662 RAP	Rapid City, S.D.
464 PUB	Pueblo, Colo.	674 COD	Cody, Wyo.
476 GJT	Grand Junction,	681 BOI	Boise, Idaho
	Colo.	688 PDT	Pendleton, Ore.
486 ELY	Ely, Nev.	693 EUG	Eugene, Ore.
488 RNO	Reno, Nev.	712 CAR	Caribou, Maine
— 493 OAK	Oakland, Calif.	745 DLH	Duluth, Minn.
503 LGA	LaGuardia Field,	753 FAR	Fargo, N.D.
	N.Y.	767 WSN	Williston, N.D.
509 BOS	Boston, Mass.	772 HLN	Helena, Mont.
518 ALB	Albany, N.Y.	777 HVR	Havre, Mont.
520 PIT	Pittsburgh, Pa.	793 SEA	Seattle, Wash.

If you draw your own base maps, you may wish to
show some southern Canadian stations on your

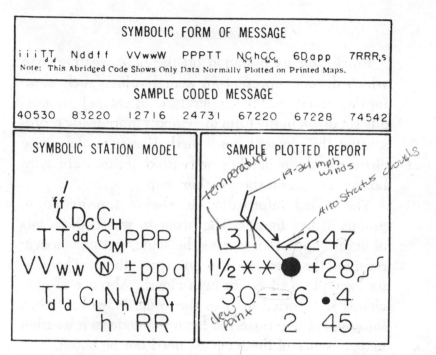

Fig. 19 Data entered on weather map. (Station circle)

weather map, especially if you live in a northern portion of the United States.

A definite arrangement of the data around the station circle is used by the Weather Bureau. It is perhaps best for you, as an amateur meteorologist, to follow this example in plotting your weather map. When the report is plotted in these fixed positions around the station circle on the weather map, many of the code figures are transcribed exactly as sent. This is shown in Figure 19.

Entries for each station on the base weather map which do not represent an actual value (such as 30 for dew point, 76 for temperature, et cetera) are usually set down in the form of symbols graphically representing the element concerned. For example, dense cirrus clouds in patches or twisted sheaves are symbolized as ⏤ᴗon the weather map.

The coded information is always transmitted in groups of five figures. The order in which these sets of figures appears is always the same, so that whoever receives the message can interpret them. There is, for example, a place for high clouds. Absence of high clouds is reported as o in the code. However, when information is transferred from the code to a weather map, absence of these clouds need not be noted.

The international code form for surface reports used by the Weather Bureau is shown in abridged form here, together with a sample message. From information contained in this sample message, two models, for one station only, are shown (Figure 19). One displays weather information, just as it is entered for each station on an entire base map. The other displays, in symbol form, the different items of weather for which this specific information is given.

Many of the elements in the sample plotted report are entered in numbers with a direct meaning, such as the 31, which indicates temperature, and 30, the dew

64

point. Some, however, require reference to code tables. This is true in the case of the Number 2, which refers to a cloud height of 300 to 599 feet.

Here is a sample coded message:

40530 83220 12716 24731 67220 67228 74542

The information contained in this message, expressed in symbolic form, is as follows:

iiiT$_d$T$_d$ Nddff VVwwW PPPTT N$_h$C$_L$hC$_M$C$_H$ 6D$_c$app 7RRR$_t$s

Set forth below are the meanings of these symbols. With this information at hand, it is then a relatively simple step to the use of Weather Bureau code tables shown on the following pages.

Explanation of symbols and form in which they are entered on weather map (Figure 19)

iii Station number: 405 (Washington, D.C.).

T$_d$T$_d$ Temperature of dew point to nearest degree Fahrenheit: 30 degrees.

N Total amount of cloud: 8 (completely covered). Observed in 10ths of cloud cover and coded in oktas (8ths), according to Code Table 5. Plotted in symbols shown in same table.

dd True direction from which wind is blowing: 32 (equals 320 degrees, or northwest). Coded in 10ths of degrees and plotted as the shaft of an arrow extending from the station circle toward the direction from which the wind is blowing.

ff Wind speed in knots: 20 (equals 20 knots, Beaufort

65

force 5). Coded in knots (nautical miles per hour) and plotted in equivalent Beaufort force as feathers and half-feathers on shaft of the wind direction arrows. See Code Table 6.

VV Visibility in miles and fractions: 12 (equals 12/8ths or 1½ miles). Coded in 8ths of miles up to 10 miles and plotted in miles and fractions. Values higher than 10 miles are omitted from the map.

ww Present weather: 71 (continuous slight snow). Coded in figures taken from the "ww" table, Code Table 9, and plotted in corresponding symbols.

W Past weather: 6 (rain). Coded in figures taken from Code Table 8 and plotted in corresponding symbols. No entries made for code figures 0, 1 or 2.

PPP Barometric pressure in millibars reduced to sea level: 247 (1024.7 mb.). Coded and plotted in tens, units and 10ths of millibars. Initial 9 or 10 and decimal point are omitted.

TT Current air temperature: 31 (31 degrees F.). Coded and plotted in actual value, whole degrees Fahrenheit.

N_h Amount of cloud whose height is reported by "h" (below): 6 (7/10ths or 8/10ths). Observed and coded same as "N." Plotted as code figure given in message. See Code Table 5.

C_L Cloud type: 7 (fractostratus and/or fractocumulus of bad weather, or scud). Predominating clouds of types listed under C_L, Code Table 1, are coded from that table and plotted in corresponding symbols.

h Height of base of cloud: 2 (300 to 599 feet). Observed in feet and coded and plotted as code figures according to Code Table 4.

66

C_M Cloud type: 2 (thick altostratus or nimbostratus). See C_L above and Code Table 1.

C_H Cloud type: 0 (no clouds C_H). See C_L above and Code Table 1.

6   Indicator figure. Not plotted.

D_C Direction of cloud movement: 7 (from the northwest). Observed in accordance with types of clouds present. Coded according to Code Table 2 and plotted adjacent to the cloud symbol to which it applies as an arrow showing direction of movement.

a   Characteristic of barograph trace: 2 (rising unsteadily). Coded according to Code Table 7 and plotted in corresponding symbols.

pp   Pressure change in 3 hours preceding observation: 28 (2.8 millibars). Coded and plotted in units and 10ths of millibars.

7   Indicator figure. Not plotted.

RR   Amount of precipitation: 45 (0.45 inches). Coded and plotted in inches and 100ths.

R_t Time precipitation began or ended: 4 (3 to 4 hours ago). Coded and plotted in figures from Code Table 3.

s   Depth of snow on ground. Ordinarily not plotted.

Data taken from the weather code is plotted for each station, as shown in the symbolic station model (Figure 19). It is usually entered in ink. When data is recorded for the desired number of stations on the base map, fronts, air mass types and isobars are plotted. Solid red lines are drawn for warm fronts and

Code Table 1

C_L

Code Number	Symbol	Description (Abridged From W.M.O. Code)
1		Cu with little vertical development and seemingly flattened.
2		Cu of considerable development, generally towering, with or without other Cu or Sc bases all at same level.
3		Cb with tops lacking clear-cut outlines, but distinctly not cirriform or anvil-shaped, with or without Cu, Sc, or St.
4		Sc formed by spreading out of Cu, Cu often present also.
5		Sc not formed by spreading out of Cu.
6		St or Fs or both, but not Fs of bad weather.
7		Fs and/or Fc of bad weather (scud) usually under As and Ns.
8		Cu and Sc (not formed by spreading out of Cu) with bases at different levels.
9		Cb having a clearly fibrous (cirriform) top, often anvil-shaped, with or without Cu, Sc, St, or scud.

C_M

Code Number	Symbol	Description (Abridged From W.M.O. Code)
1		Thin As (entire cloud layer semitransparent).
2		Thick As, or Ns.
3		Thin Ac, cloud elements not changing much and at a single level.
4		Thin Ac in patches; cloud elements continually changing and/or occurring at more than one level.
5		Thin Ac in bands or in a layer gradually spreading over sky and usually thickening as a whole.
6		Ac formed by the spreading out of Cu.
7		Double-layered Ac or a thick layer of Ac, not increasing, or As and Ac both present at same or different levels.
8		Ac in the form of Cu-shaped tufts or Ac with turrets.
9		Ac of a chaotic sky, usually at different levels, patches of dense Ci are usually present also.

C_H

Code Number	Symbol	Description (Abridged From W.M.O. Code)
1		Filaments of Ci, scattered and not increasing.
2		Dense Ci in patches or twisted sheaves, usually not increasing.
3		Ci, often anvil-shaped, derived from or associated with Cb.
4		Ci, often hook-shaped, gradually spreading over the sky and usually thickening as a whole.
5		Ci and Cs, often in converging bands, or Cs alone; the continuous layer not reaching 45° altitude.
6		Ci and Cs, often in converging bands, or Cs alone; the continuous layer exceeding 45° altitude.
7		Cs covering the entire sky.
8		Cs not increasing and not covering entire sky; Ci and Cc may be present.
9		Cc alone or Cc with some Ci or Cs, but the Cc being the main cirriform cloud present.

Code Table 1

Cloud Abbreviation	Code Number	D_c	Cloud Direction
St or Fs-Stratus or Fractostratus	0	NONE	No Clouds, or Calm
Ci-Cirrus	1	↙	Northeast
Cs-Cirrostratus	2	←	East
Cc-Cirrocumulus	3	↖	Southeast
Ac-Altocumulus	4	↑	South
As-Altostratus	5	↗	Southwest
Sc-Stratocumulus	6	→	West
Ns-Nimbostratus	7	↘	Northwest
Cu or Fc-Cumulus or Fractocumulus	8	↓	North
Cb-Cumulonimbus	9	NONE	Unknown, or Variable

Code Table 2

R_t	Time of Precipitation
0	No Precipitation
1	Less than 1 hour ago
2	1 to 2 hours ago
3	2 to 3 hours ago
4	3 to 4 hours ago
5	4 to 5 hours ago
6	5 to 6 hours ago
7	6 to 12 hours ago
8	More than 12 hours ago
9	Unknown

Code Table 3

69

h	Height in Feet (Rounded Off)	Height in Meters (Approximate)
0	0 - 149	0 - 49
1	150 - 299	50 - 99
2	300 - 599	100 - 199
3	600 - 999	200 - 299
4	1,000-1,999	300 - 599
5	2,000-3,499	600 - 999
6	3,500-4,999	1,000-1,499
7	5,000-6,499	1,500-1,999
8	6,500-7,999	2,000-2,499
9	At or above 8,000, or no clouds	At or above 2,500, or no clouds

N	N$_h$	Sky Coverage
	0	No clouds.
	1	Less than one-tenth or one-tenth.
	2	Two- or three-tenths.
	3	Four-tenths.
	4	Five-tenths.
	5	Six-tenths.
	6	Seven- or eight-tenths.
	7	Nine-tenths or overcast with openings.
	8	Completely overcast.
	9	Sky obscured.

Code Table 4   .   **Code Table 5**

Beaufort Number	ff	Miles (Statute) Per Hour	Knots	Beaufort Number	ff	Miles (Statute) Per Hour	Knots
0		Calm	Calm	9		47-54	41-47
1		1-3	1-3	10		55-63	48-55
2		4-7	4-6	11		64-72	56-63
3		8-12	7-10	12		73-82	64-71
4		13-18	11-16	13		83-92	72-80
5		19-24	17-21	14		93-103	81-89
6		25-31	22-27	15		104-114	90-99
7		32-38	28-33	16		115-125	100-108
8		39-46	34-40	17		126-136	109-118

Code Table 6: Beaufort Wind Scale

Code Number	a	Barometric Tendency	
0		Rising, then falling.	
1		Rising, then steady; or rising, then rising more slowly.	
2		Rising unsteadily, or unsteady.	Barometer now higher than, or same as, 3 hours ago.
3		Rising steadily, or steady. (not plotted)	
4		Falling or steady, then rising; or rising, then rising more quickly.	
5		Falling, then rising.	
6		Falling, then steady; or falling, then falling more slowly.	
7		Falling unsteadily, or unsteady.	Barometer now lower than 3 hours ago.
8		Falling Steadily. (not plotted)	
9		Steady or rising, then falling; or falling, then falling more quickly.	

Code Table 7

Code Number	W	Past weather	
0		Clear or few clouds	
1		Partly cloudy (scattered) or variable sky.	Not Plotted
2		Cloudy (broken) or overcast.	
3		Sandstorm, or dust-storm, or drifting or blowing snow.	
4		Fog, or smoke, or thick dust haze.	
5		Drizzle.	
6		Rain.	
7		Snow, or rain and snow mixed, or ice pellets (sleet).	
8		Shower(s).	
9		Thunderstorm, with or without precipitation.	

Code Table 8

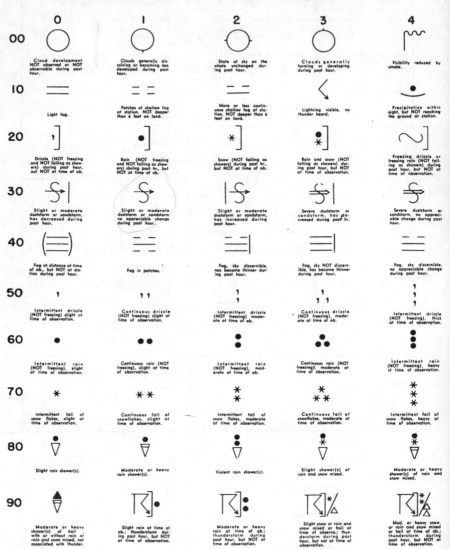

	0	1	2	3	4
00	Cloud development NOT observed or NOT observable during past hour.	Clouds generally dissolving or becoming less developed during past hour.	State of sky on the whole unchanged during past hour.	Clouds generally forming or developing during past hour.	Visibility reduced by smoke.
10	Light fog.	Patches of shallow fog at station, NOT deeper than 6 feet on land.	More or less continuous shallow fog at station, NOT deeper than 6 feet on land.	Lightning visible, no thunder heard.	Precipitation within sight, but NOT reaching the ground at station.
20	Drizzle (NOT freezing and NOT falling as showers) during past hour, but NOT at time of ob.	Rain (NOT freezing and NOT falling as showers) during past hr., but NOT at time of ob.	Snow (NOT falling as showers) during past hr., but NOT at time of ob.	Rain and snow (NOT falling as showers) during past hour, but NOT at time of observation.	Freezing drizzle or freezing rain (NOT falling as showers) during past hour, but NOT at time of observation.
30	Slight or moderate duststorm or sandstorm, has decreased during past hour.	Slight or moderate duststorm or sandstorm no appreciable change during past hour.	Slight or moderate duststorm or sandstorm has increased during past hour.	Severe duststorm or sandstorm, has decreased during past hr.	Severe duststorm or sandstorm, no appreciable change during past hour.
40	Fog at distance at time of ob., but NOT at station during past hour.	Fog in patches.	Fog, sky discernible, has become thinner during past hour.	Fog, sky NOT discernible, has become thinner during past hour.	Fog, sky discernible, no appreciable change during past hour.
50	Intermittent drizzle (NOT freezing) slight at time of observation.	Continuous drizzle (NOT freezing) slight at time of observation.	Intermittent drizzle (NOT freezing) moderate at time of ob.	Continuous drizzle (NOT freezing), moderate at time of ob.	Intermittent drizzle (NOT freezing), thick at time of observation.
60	Intermittent rain (NOT freezing), slight at time of observation.	Continuous rain (NOT freezing), slight at time of observation.	Intermittent rain (NOT freezing), moderate at time of ob.	Continuous rain (NOT freezing), moderate at time of observation.	Intermittent rain (NOT freezing), heavy at time of observation.
70	Intermittent fall of snow flakes, slight at time of observation.	Continuous fall of snowflakes, slight at time of observation.	Intermittent fall of snow flakes, moderate at time of observation.	Continuous fall of snowflakes, moderate at time of observation.	Intermittent fall of snow flakes, heavy at time of observation.
80	Slight rain shower(s).	Moderate or heavy rain shower(s).	Violent rain shower(s).	Slight shower(s) of rain and snow mixed.	Moderate or heavy shower(s) of rain and snow mixed.
90	Moderate or heavy shower(s) of hail, with or without rain or rain and snow mixed, not associated with thunder.	Slight rain at time of ob.; thunderstorm during past hour, but NOT at time of observation.	Moderate or heavy rain at time of ob.; thunderstorm during past hour, but NOT at time of observation.	Slight snow or rain and snow mixed or hail at time of observa.; thunderstorm during past hour, but not at time of observation.	Mod. or heavy snow, or rain and snow mixed or hail at time of ob.; thunderstorm during past hour, but NOT at time of observation.

Code Table 9

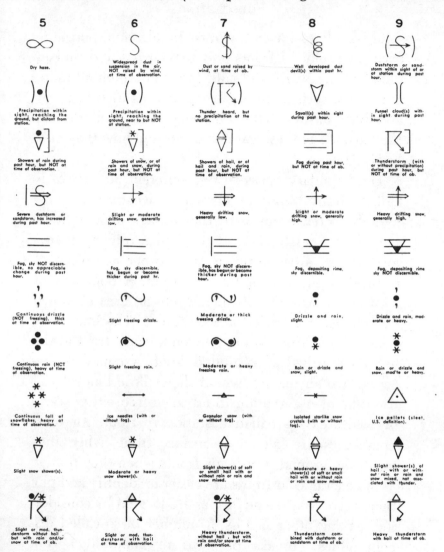

5	6	7	8	9
Dry haze.	Widespread dust in suspension in the air, NOT raised by wind, at time of observation.	Dust or sand raised by wind, at time of ob.	Well developed dust devil(s) within past hr.	Duststorm or sandstorm within sight of or at station during past hour.
Precipitation within sight, reaching the ground, but distant from station.	Precipitation within sight, reaching the ground, near to but NOT at station.	Thunder heard, but no precipitation at the station.	Squall(s) within sight during past hour.	Funnel cloud(s) within sight during past hour.
Showers of rain during past hour, but NOT at time of observation.	Showers of snow, or of rain and snow, during past hour, but NOT at time of observation.	Showers of hail, or of hail and rain, during past hour, but NOT at time of observation.	Fog during past hour, but NOT at time of ob.	Thunderstorm (with or without precipitation) during past hour, but NOT at time of ob.
Severe duststorm or sandstorm, has increased during past hour.	Slight or moderate drifting snow, generally low.	Heavy drifting snow, generally low.	Slight or moderate drifting snow, generally high.	Heavy drifting snow, generally high.
Fog, sky NOT discernible, no appreciable change during past hour.	Fog, sky discernible, has begun or become thicker during past hr.	Fog, sky NOT discernible, has begun or become thicker during past hour.	Fog, depositing rime, sky discernible.	Fog, depositing rime, sky NOT discernible.
Continuous drizzle (NOT freezing), thick at time of observation.	Slight freezing drizzle.	Moderate or thick freezing drizzle.	Drizzle and rain, slight.	Drizzle and rain, moderate or heavy.
Continuous rain (NCT freezing), heavy at time of observation.	Slight freezing rain.	Moderate or heavy freezing rain.	Rain or drizzle and snow, slight.	Rain or drizzle and snow, mod'te or heavy.
Continuous fall of snowflakes, heavy at time of observation.	Ice needles (with or without fog).	Granular snow (with or without fog).	Isolated starlike snow crystals (with or without fog).	Ice pellets (sleet, U.S. definition).
Slight snow shower(s).	Moderate or heavy snow shower(s).	Slight shower(s) of soft or small hail with or without rain or rain and snow mixed.	Moderate or heavy shower(s) of soft or small hail with or without rain or rain and snow mixed.	Slight shower(s) of hail, with or without rain or rain and snow mixed, not associated with thunder.
Slight or mod. thunderstorm without hail, but with rain and/or snow at time of ob.	Slight or mod. thunderstorm, with hail at time of observation.	Heavy thunderstorm, without hail, but with rain and/or snow at time of observation.	Thunderstorm combined with duststorm or sandstorm at time of observation.	Heavy thunderstorm with hail at time of ob.

Code Table 9

73

solid blue lines for cold fronts. In addition, purple is used for occluded fronts and broken red and broken blue lines for warm and cold fronts at a high altitude. Stationary surface fronts are drawn as alternate red and blue dashes. The following pages will discuss the meaning of these various fronts and how they may be recognized.

The boundary between two different air masses is called a front. Important changes in weather and temperature often occur with the passage of a front. A boundary of relatively cold air of polar origin, advancing into an area occupied by warmer air, often of tropical origin, is called a cold front. A boundary of relatively warm air, advancing into an area occupied by colder air, is called a warm front. The line along which a cold front has overtaken a warm front at the ground is called an occluded front. A boundary between two air masses, which shows little tendency at the time of observation to advance into either warm or cold areas, is called a stationary front. Air mass boundaries are known as surface fronts when they touch the ground; upper air fronts when they do not.

In general, cold fronts are easier to identify and plot than warm fronts. The former are located by considering, among other factors, a number of so-called discontinuities (breaks or gaps in continuity). For example, if the temperature in Omaha, Nebraska, is

74

82 degrees, and at North Platte, Nebraska, it is only 65 degrees, this discontinuity in temperature would be an indication of a cold front at some location between the two cities. There are other discontinuities that enter into the picture also—in dew point and surface winds. Likewise factors in locating a front are pressure tendencies and characteristics, type of clouds and kind of precipitation, if any. Recollection of how other cold fronts have developed over a particular area can also be valuable in the identification of succeeding fronts. When temperature and wind discontinuities are well-marked, locating a cold front becomes easy. But when there is little temperature difference between the warm sector and a colder air mass to the west, barometric tendencies and other aids must be used. Steadily rising pressure is characteristic of a cold front and the area immediately behind it. Often the amount is quite marked. Farther behind the front, the pressure still shows a rising tendency, although not so great. In considering wind discontinuities at the cold front, colder air may be carried by winds from any westerly quarter, even southwest (although normally, a southwest wind is a warm one).

The main reason why warm fronts, as a rule, are harder to locate is that the enveloping warm air mixes quickly with cool air at slight elevations. Since cool air generally exists as a very thin layer hugging the surface of the earth, the overrunning warm air quickly modifies both its temperature and dew point and in turn has its own temperature and dew point modified. Wind discontinuity is also poorly marked, as a rule. Rain or other precipitation, a short distance ahead of a warm front, often serves to place the front approximately. Also, ahead of a warm front the barometer shows a steadily falling tendency, while in the warm sector immediately back of the front, pressure drop is much less. In this connection, also, at upper air levels it is possible to identify the front by noting the line between stations showing barometer readings that are falling and those that are steady or rising. The advance of this line of divergence often approximates the progress of a warm front. There are still other methods of identifying warm fronts. For example, a warm front moving in, at a high altitude, can be detected by noting the presence of altostratus clouds; at higher levels, by cirrostratus and cirrus. Frequently the difference between dew point and current temperature will be of help.

Isobars, or lines of equal barometric pressure, are customarily drawn in black on the weather map. If, for example, several stations reported a barometer reading of 1020 millibars, these points would be connected by an isobar. Since barometric pressure is reported in millibars (a millibar is a unit of pressure equal to

76

approximately 3/100ths of an inch of mercury; inversely, there are approximately 34 millibars to the
inch) and tenths, however, the chances of a number
of stations reporting a reading of 1020 are slim. There-
fore, the 1020 millibar line is drawn between stations
reporting somewhat lower or higher pressures than
1020. Isobars may be drawn at intervals of 3 millibars
—for example, 1014, 1017, 1020, 1023, etc. Isobars
outline atmospheric disturbances and locate their
centers (the highs and lows). They, along with fronts,
are the most prominent features on the weather map.

Figure 20 shows a portion of a weather map. In
this drawing, only fronts and isobars are drawn. Black
dots are station locations and numbers to the right of
each one are barometric pressures for these stations.

Fig. 20 Drawing isobars

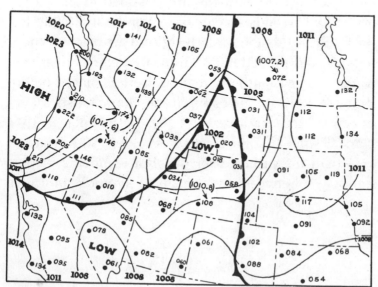

Only the last three numbers are shown—just as pressure is sent in the weather code. An actual pressure of 1014.6 would be transmitted as 146; 996.7 would be 967, etc.

Isobars connect all points of equal pressure but do not necessarily pass through a particular station. If you use 3-millibar intervals on your map, the 1011 isobar would pass between two adjacent stations reporting 1009.6 and 1012.2 millibars respectively. In other words, interpolation is used. Isobars are usually drawn for pressures of 999, 1002, 1005, 1008, and so on. The Washington weather map shows isobars at 5-millibar intervals—995, 1000, 1005, etc.

Areas of precipitation and fog may be shaded in with light green or yellow pencil, or cross-hatching may be used. Figures 26 and 27 show this.

Masses of air of differing characteristics, as they move across the continent, are classified to show their origin and basic characteristics. For example, the letter P (Polar) denotes relatively cold air from northern regions, and the letter T (Tropical) denotes relatively warm air from southerly regions. Letters placed before P and T indicate air of maritime characteristics (m) or continental characteristics (c). Letters placed after P and T show that the air mass is colder (k) or warmer (w) than the surface over which it is moving. A plus sign (+) between two air mass symbols indicates

78

mixed air masses, and an arrow ($\rightarrow$) between two symbols indicates a transitional air mass changing from one type to another. Two air mass symbols, one above the other and separated by a line, indicate one air mass aloft and another at lower levels. To sum up, it will be noted that air mass symbols are formed from the following letters: m—maritime; c—continental; A —arctic; P—polar; T—tropical; S—superior (a warm, dry air mass having its origin aloft); k—colder; and w—warmer (than the surface over which the air mass is moving). While nothing in the weather map code specifically gives this information, it may be filled in on the weather map after the fronts and isobars have been located.

We have merely touched on air mass types and fronts here, as a guide to drawing weather maps. These will be gone into more fully on succeeding pages.

Weather maps drawn by professionals should be studied for correct map construction. Especially helpful in this respect is the printed Washington weather map. Fronts on this map are not printed in color. A symbolic black and white form is used instead. An explanation of these front symbols and all other symbols used is included with each Sunday's weather map.

Before going into forecasting from weather maps, it might be well to mention a way to obtain weather information on a regional basis that is quite useful to the amateur meteorologist. As previously mentioned, airways Weather Bureau offices take hourly observations and put them on teletype circuits. These observations are not as complete as the six-hourly map observations, but they contain information suitable especially for pilots.

Many CAA stations broadcast these reports for a selected number of their own stations in the area, sometimes covering regular air routes in several adjoining states. Broadcasts are made over regular longwave radio range stations on frequencies between 200 and 400 kilocycles. They may also be carried simultaneously over VHF omni-range frequencies and other radio aids to aviation. The weather information is transmitted in plain language and broadcasts are made at 15 and 45 minutes past the hour. A typical observation for one station might sound like this in the broadcast:

Des Moines: Ceiling 8,000 feet, overcast, visibility 8 miles, light rain, temperature 56, dew point 54, wind south-southwest 18 miles per hour.

Observations for eight or ten other stations in the area may be given. Altimeter setting for the station originating the broadcast is given, but not for other stations. Altimeter settings are given in inches of mercury and are very close to the sea level barometer reading for the station. The altimeter setting is used for setting a pressure-scale type sensitive altimeter in an airplane so that when the plane lands, the instrument will indicate an altitude reading equal or very close to that of the airfield's elevation above sea level. Formerly, altimeter settings for all stations included in the broadcast were given, making it possible to draw a regional weather map complete with isobars showing position of highs and lows. Information given at present is mainly valuable for showing position and progress of fronts, cloud conditions, thunderstorms, et cetera.

Many commercial receivers and some portable sets have the radio-range band on their dials. It is also possible to build a simple receiver for picking up weather broadcasts. At the time of this writing, there are several types of war surplus receivers advertised in the popular radio magazines covering the radio-range frequencies, some of them costing as little as six dollars.

Elements of Scientific Forecasting

The sun's rays as they reach the earth are partly absorbed, mostly in the lower layers of the atmosphere. Rays which are not absorbed are reflected from the earth and serve to warm the moist layers of air close to the earth's surface. A second warming influence on

81

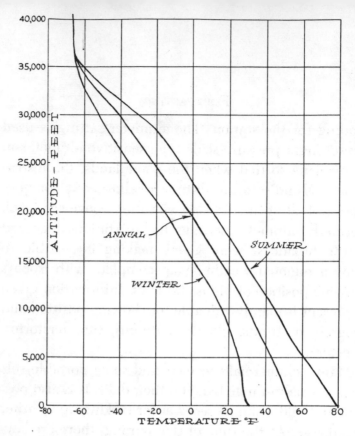

Fig. 21 Mean free-air temperature at latitude 40° N. in the United States.

these moist layers of air is the heat which has been absorbed by the actual surface of the earth and then radiated back into space. It can be deduced from this that the earth's atmosphere is warmest in its lower regions and normally the temperature decreases with elevation. Figure 21 shows the average height-temperature relationship at latitude 40° N. in the United States.

82

If a portion of surface air is warmed, it becomes lighter than the surrounding air and is forced to rise. As it rises, pressure on it becomes less and it expands. As it expands, it "does work"—that is, pushes aside surrounding air and loses some heat. Ascending dry air cools at an average rate of 1° Fahrenheit per 180 feet of ascent.

On the other hand, when air from high levels descends because it is heavier than air masses around it, the increasing pressure compresses it. In this case the surrounding air is doing work on the descending body of air and its temperature rises at about 1° Fahrenheit per 180 feet of descent.

If the ascending and descending action described above were continuous and this were the only factor to consider, the rate of 1° Fahrenheit per 180 feet would always hold true. However, there are other factors to consider. Sometimes on quiet nights, the earth radiates a great amount of heat, resulting in a lowering of the air temperature near the surface. In this case, the temperature may *increase* with elevation for some distance. This is called a temperature "inversion."

Water surfaces reflect more of the sun's heat than does land. However, some of the sun's rays do penetrate deep into the water and are absorbed. A larger amount of heat is required to heat a given amount of water a given number of degrees than is the case with any other substance.

Water heats and cools more slowly than land. Consequently, temperature changes are more rapid over land surfaces. One effect of this difference in temperature change rates is land and sea breezes.

Thus we see that radiation from the sun results in unequal heating in different areas on the earth's surface.

The greatest amount of heating on the earth's surface is, logically, at the equator. This hot air rises to a height of about 10 miles and flows outward to the north and south. This flowing hot air cools as it travels toward the poles and becomes more dense. A large portion of it descends in tropical regions and flows back to the equator. The remainder continues flowing toward the poles, being deflected in an easterly direction owing to the earth's rotation. It is this poleward wind movement that results in the "prevailing westerlies" in the north and south temperate zones.

As the wind flow traverses the temperate zones, the effect of the earth's rotation on it gradually decreases. The upper wind which finally reaches the poles settles on the earth's surface and creates a polar high-pressure area. Winds then blow out from the poles (toward the southeast in the northern hemisphere). At a latitude of approximately 60°, the cold polar winds en-

84

counter the prevailing westerlies. The polar air, being cold, is stopped or "dammed up." When a quantity of it collects, a mass of it may then push into more southerly latitudes. The boundary of this mass of cold air is a "polar front," or cold front of the weather map.

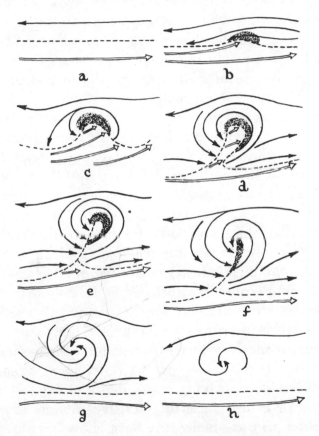

Fig. 22 The sequence a, b, c, etc., shows the formation of a wave disturbance (a and b) on the boundary between a cold and warm current; development of a low pressure area (c and d); occlusion (e and f); and dissipation (g and h)

Up to now we have touched only briefly on two weather terms that are of paramount importance—high barometric pressure areas and low barometric pressure areas, or the "highs" and "lows" of the weather map. When you draw isobars on a weather map, you are outlining these areas of highs and lows. When you draw wind direction arrows on the weather map, you are further identifying these highs and lows. This is true because in the northern hemisphere, surface winds generally circulate spirally in a clockwise direction outward for highs and a counter-clockwise direction toward the center for lows. This is shown in detail in Figure 22. Like nearly every phase of weather, there is no hard and fast rule about this, since the wind might be deflected by hills or other local conditions. However, even these local influences are of little consequence when a low becomes intense.

Actually, highs and lows are not weather-makers but reflect weather in the making. Cold air accompanying the high is heavier than warm air because it is denser. Because it is heavier, it follows that cold air exerts more pressure on the instrument used to measure this pressure—the barometer. This sends the column of mercury in the barometer higher—hence, the term "High." Heat, on the other hand, expands the atmosphere, making it less dense or lighter. The lighter air cannot raise the mercury column as high as colder air can—hence, the term "Low."

86

While these changes in barometric pressure are extremely significant to the weather forecaster, they are in themselves not very great. Seldom does a barometer change as much as one inch (34 millibars) in 24 hours. When it does, it's a good bet there's a storm moving in rapidly.

In fact, it's generally a good bet that stormy weather is in the offing when the barometer drops steadily. This drop shows the approach or development of a low.

While storms can develop anywhere, they seem to follow certain general paths. Figure 23 shows their origins and average paths in winter.

If an observer could equip himself with a barometer, wind vane and psychrometer, plus a rapid means of transportation, then flit about the country at will and at the speed of light, he would be in for an amazing treat. Suppose he started on this imaginary journey at New York City on a day in December. His barometer might read 30.40 inches (or 1029.5 millibars); his thermometer, 26 degrees. Perhaps it is clear, with a southeast wind blowing, and the relative humidity is 45%.

From New York City our superman decides to jump to Chicago, there to take an observation one minute later than the one he made in New York City. In a flash, he is there! But in Chicago, the temperature is

87

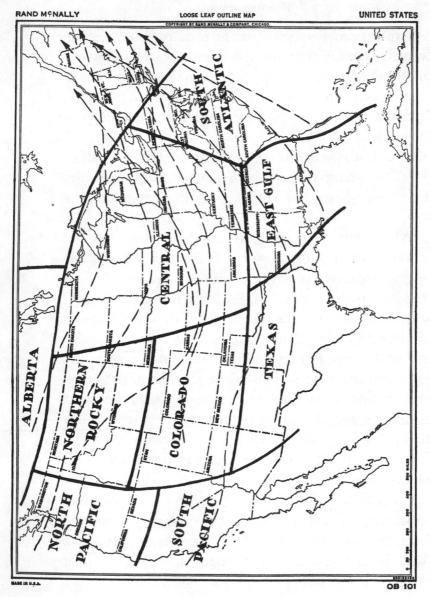

Fig. 23 Average January storm paths in the United States and the regions of their origins.

29 degrees and his barometer reads 29.80 (we're assuming a reduction to sea level for all pressures). A moderate snow is falling, wind is blowing from the southwest, and the relative humidity is 98%. Our observer has traveled so fast, he did not see high cirrus clouds as he winged over Pennsylvania, or, in eastern Ohio, stratus clouds and the beginning of snowfall. Had he lingered in Ohio for a little while, he might also have watched his wind vane swing from southeast around to southwest as a warm front moved across that state.

Having scanned the sky in Chicago, our mythical friend jumps instantly to Omaha. In that eastern Nebraska city, fine snow is being driven from the northwest in the teeth of a gale-like wind; the barometer reads 30.20 and is rising so fast you can almost see it go up. Our meteorological messenger might rest a while in Omaha, and in those few hours he notes the sky clearing and wind velocity dropping a little.

The weather which our fast traveler observed first-hand on his quick trip across half a continent would have looked like this, had it been plotted on a weather map: A high-pressure area, with dry, cool air, was moving into the North Atlantic, having been centered just south of New York City the day before. Streaming up from the South was a body or mass of comparatively warm, moist air. Its boundary, or front, had

89

reached central Ohio and extended southeastward across North Carolina. Probably some rain was falling along this front at its southern end, with snow farther north. Somewhere over the Great Lakes, at the extreme northern end of this front, was a point of very low barometric pressure—the center of a cyclonic storm, or low-pressure area.

But still another force was in the picture. Extending down from the land of incessant snow and intense cold was a mass of cold air—fighting, pushing against the warm air mass. Cold air is dense and heavy, and a barometer reading in the center of this cold air mass would be high. This would be the center of an anticyclone—the high of the weather map. At the front of this push of cold air, we would draw a heavy blue line on the weather map—a cold front.

For this is the story of weather, the constant battle of masses of air from different source regions, the fronts or barriers between, and the attendant high- and low-pressure areas.

Weather, as shown on a weather map, is a dynamic thing, an ever-moving array of highs and lows, fronts and air masses, clouds and precipitation, traveling generally from west to east across the country. With a weather map in front of us, we can scan the country as fast as our friend might have moved from point to point—faster, in fact, because we can learn to take in a whole continent at a glance and make a forecast from the picture we see.

Before going into the principles of air-mass analysis and forecasting, it might be well to insert here some of the physical processes involved in the production of clouds and precipitation.

We have explained the process of condensation in an earlier section of this book. Dew, frost, rain, snow, hail and sleet are all condensed moisture. With the exception of dew and frost, all these forms of precipitation are the result of condensation in the upper air.

Clouds form when air is lifted and cools below the dew point. Minute droplets form on microscopic particles—condensation nuclei. These droplets are light enough to be supported by the air and float or fall very slowly. When air is lifted by processes described later, condensation and clouds result.

Cloud droplets must increase tremendously in order to fall as precipitation. In one process, when upper cloud areas reach a sub-freezing altitude, the droplets super-cool—that is, they remain liquid although below a freezing temperature. As the cloud grows even higher, some of the droplets freeze and moisture from adjacent liquid droplets will condense on them. As the now heavier droplets begin to fall, they collect more moisture by collision and coalescence. If the temperature is freezing all the way to the ground, the precipitation falls as snow. If air below the cloud is above freezing, the snowflakes will melt and fall to the earth as rain.

Droplets will sometimes coalesce without the freezing process and fall as rain. This condition usually exists in stratus-type clouds.

If the air below a precipitation cloud is dry, the rain or snow may partially or completely evaporate before it reaches the ground. These wisps of evaporating precipitation, sometimes seen trailing below the clouds (especially in arid regions), are known as virga.

The term "sleet" is applied when raindrops pass through a layer of cold air and freeze before they reach the ground. Glaze is the result when rain falls upon sub-freezing ground surfaces.

As mentioned before, various types of air masses move across the country from their source regions— cold, dry air from the polar regions and warm, moist air from the Gulf and Pacific areas. These masses of air are characterized by their temperature in relation to the temperature of the surface over which they pass. Thus a cold air mass in summer may actually have surface temperatures no lower than 65 degrees. But since it has come from Northern Canada and maintains its identity, we would designate it as continental polar cold air. Masses of air (the relatively cold, dry ones and the relatively warm, moist ones) maintain their characteristics for long periods as they travel across the country. Eventually they are modified as they pass into different regions and finally lose their identity. It is at the boundaries of these air masses, the more or less well-defined separations between them, the fronts, that storms and precipitation occur.

Low-pressure areas, the lows, are formed by a disturbance and wave action at a point between two air masses, as shown in Figure 22 A spiraling wind movement sets in and the cyclonic action develops. As long as the source energy is maintained, the low continues to gain in force and more or less precipitation falls along the fronts or air mass boundaries. As warm, moist air flows into the low, it is lifted above the colder, denser air and its moisture is condensed out, forming clouds and ultimately rain or snow. These masses of warm and cold air are separated by boundary lines, or fronts. The cold front shows where cold air is replacing warm air, and the warm front where cold air is being replaced by warm.

Figure 24 shows two cross sections through an idealized low, one north of the center and the other in the southern sector. Shaded areas show where precipitation may be expected in relation to warm and cold fronts. As a warm front advances, a compara-

93

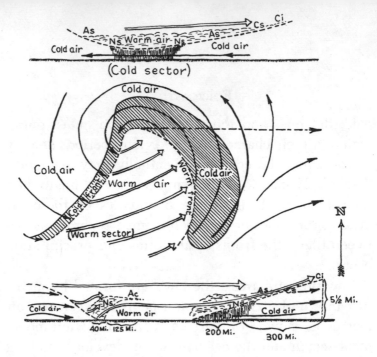

Fig. 24 Low pressure area formed by the process illustrated in Figure 22 with vertical east-west cross sections through the northern part (*above*) and the southern part (*below*). (*After Bjerknes*)

tively large area of clouds and precipitation fans out in advance of it. The precipitation area in relation to a cold front is usually narrow and of short duration at any particular point.

When a cold air mass advances rapidly, the warm sector of a low is literally squeezed between it and the cold air ahead. Warm air is pushed aloft. Advancing cold air may push under the air ahead of the front and a cold front occlusion will ensue, with the greatest amount of rain or snow falling behind the surface

94

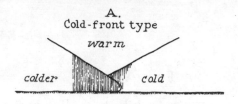

A.
Cold-front type

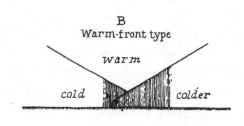

B
Warm-front type

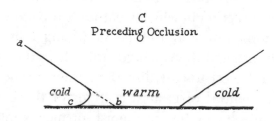

C
Preceding Occlusion

Fig. 25 Types of occlusions.

front. If cold air advancing from the rear is not as cold as the air it overtakes, it will slide over the colder air mass in front. This is known as a warm front-type occlusion, and the most precipitation usually falls ahead of this surface front.

When two cold air masses have about the same temperature, a neutral-type occlusion results. Some precipitation may occur along this front but the low-pressure system soon dissipates.

Lows follow a regular life history—they form, increase in intensity for a while, then die out. Sometimes they form in *groups* on fronts separating polar air from warm, moist air.

A well-drawn weather map will show position of highs, lows, fronts, areas of precipitation, et cetera. It is then up to the forecaster to determine where these highs, lows, fronts and areas of rain and snow will be at midnight, or the next day, or some other period of time. Among items to be considered are speed and direction in which weather is traveling, plus effect of topography and other modifying influences.

Areas of precipitation change radically as they move in a general west-to-east direction. Rain attending a low in the central or eastern sections of the country may be quite heavy because moist air moves into the low from the Gulf region. A day or two earlier, precipitation attending this same low may have been very scant when the low was centered in the arid western slope region of the country. This is because moist Pacific air currents have their moisture condensed and rained out as they rise over the Cascade mountains.

As mentioned before, the general movement of weather is in an easterly direction. But this movement may sometimes be modified and, indeed, lows may move erratically at times, especially in the spring.

A large percentage of lows and their attendant air masses and fronts move across the United States along

96

the northern border. Others move farther south and pick up moisture from the Gulf. As they move, they increase in intensity. Lows that move from southwest regions northeastward toward the Atlantic coast are usually the most intense and bring heavy rain or snow to the central and eastern states because they are supplied with a rich source of moisture from the Gulf.

The speed at which lows move across the country is hard to predict. Sometimes they travel fast; at other times they slow down and even stop for a period of time. The forecaster trying to determine the future of a particular low utilizes such information as speed and direction of previous lows, movement of upper air currents and pressure changes.

But predicting the future position of a low is only part of the problem. The forecaster wants to know where, and how much, precipitation will fall, temperature changes, and amount and type of cloudiness as the storm area progresses. Upper air information, obtained from radiosonde instruments, is a great help to the forecaster in anticipating progress of a low system. The radiosonde is an instrument carried aloft by a balloon, which transmits pressure, temperature and relative humidity to a ground receiving-station. Some of the data received is shown on the Washington weather map, and radiosonde reports for many stations are broadcast by WEK and WSY. Another help

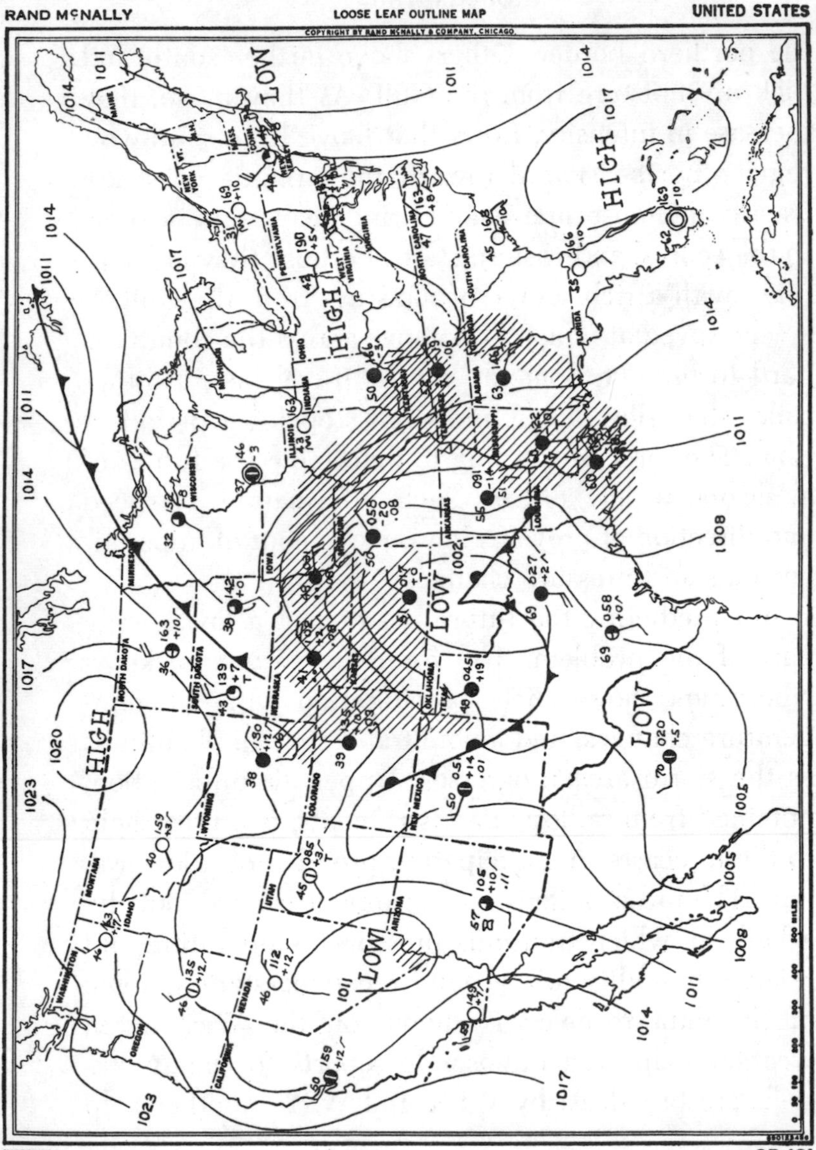

Fig. 26. Weather Map A

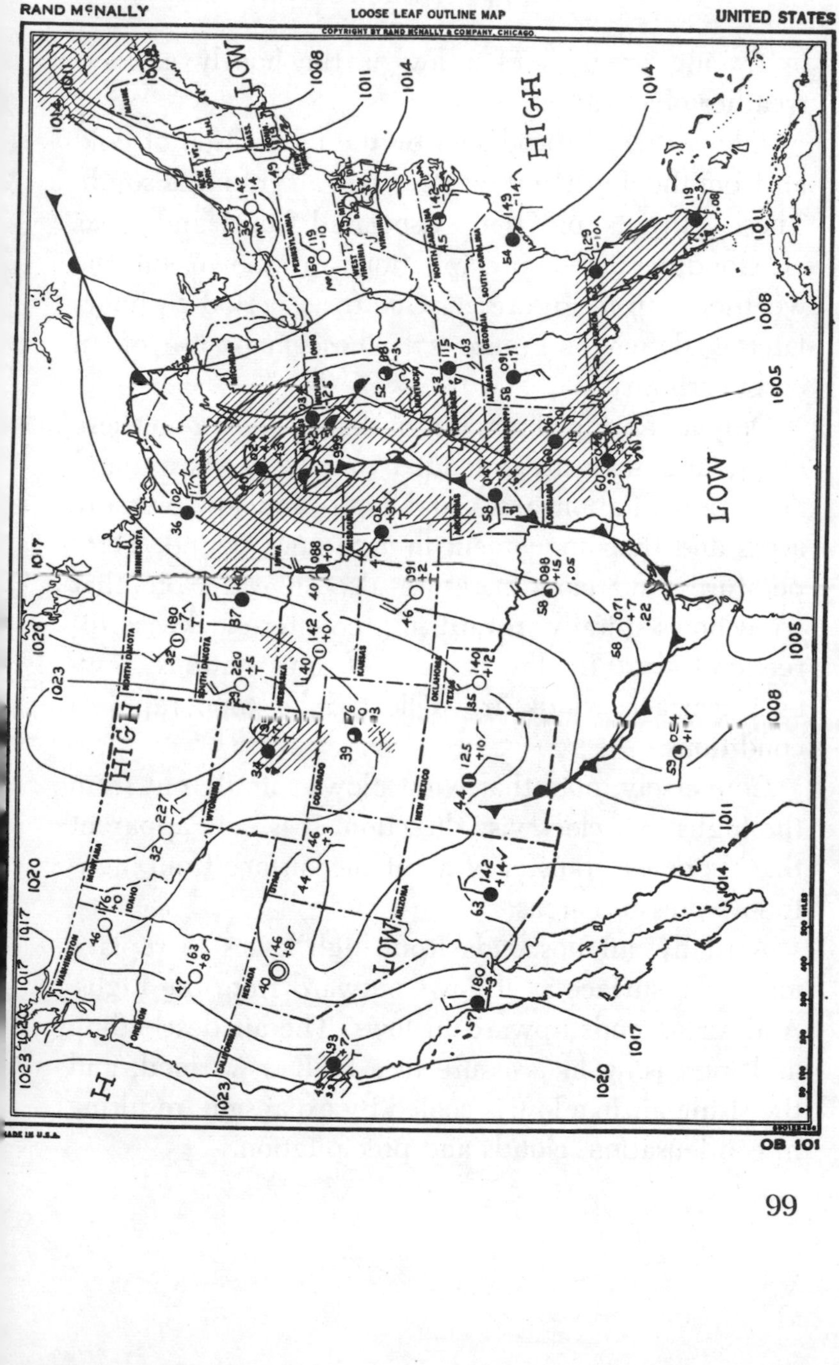

Fig. 27 Weather Map B

99

in tracing progress of a low is the hourly airways weather observation.

A low, then, is produced by the interaction of cold air from the north and warm, moist air from the south. These currents and their associated fronts and areas of cloudiness and precipitation are shown on the weather map in Figure 26. One for a period 24 hours later is shown in Figure 27. These maps are of an early spring type.

Only an abridged amount of data is shown on these maps, and they are intended mainly to show wind flow, precipitation areas and high- and low-pressure areas and their movement in a 24-hour period. Temperatures and cloudiness are also shown. Note that wind flows spirally inward in a counter-clockwise direction toward the low centers. At some stations, however, surface winds are deflected by topographical conditions.

Conversely, note that wind blows spirally out from the highs in a clockwise direction. It is now apparent that there is a transfer of air at the surface from high- to low-pressure areas.

Actually, air descends from high levels to replace air at the surface as it flows outward from the highs. And air ascends upward in lows. The air descending and increasing in pressure in a high is warmed, and the rising air in a low is cooled by expansion, resulting in condensation, clouds and precipitation.

Note the fronts in conjunction with the low centered over Oklahoma in Figure 26. Differences in wind direction on opposite sides of the front are evident. Temperature differences in the warm and cold sectors are also well-marked.

Precipitation, drawn as a shaded area, is the result of warm, moist air from the Gulf moving north and west. It has lifted and cooled, causing condensation and finally precipitation.

Figure 27 shows how the low has advanced and intensified. Wind speeds are higher. The following high is stronger. Its cold air mass and preceding front have reached the Gulf.

Once again it must be pointed out that accuracy in weather forecasting depends, first of all, upon a constant study of weather maps and watching the development, progress and results of weather types. Forecasting might be called a combination of art and science.

Thunderstorms: We have discussed generally the study of air masses and low- and high-pressure systems. One of the most difficult of weather phenomena to forecast as to time, place and intensity is the thunderstorm. The thunderstorm, with its turbulent air currents, rain, lightning and massive towering cumulus clouds, is one of the most spectacular of all weather phenomena.

Thunderstorms may occur under several different atmospheric conditions, as shown on the weather map. One of the common types is the air mass thunderstorm, or local type. These storms are the result of convection—rising warm air currents caused by local heating. They may occur during the summer in any type of air mass, but are most common in warm, moist tropical Gulf air. Air-mass thunderstorms usually develop on warm, humid summer afternoons. Cumulus clouds seem to boil upward and those receiving the most convective energy rise to great heights.

Most violent thunderstorms occur in connection with cold fronts. These are the squall-line type of storm. They are caused by the pushing up of warm air by an advancing cold front. Cold-front thunderstorms may be classified as prefrontal, frontal or postfrontal, depending on whether they occur ahead of, at, or behind the front. The prefrontal type is due to the uplifting of warm air ahead of a cold front. Those occurring along the front are due to normal frontal uplifting. Storms that develop behind the front are apparently an air-mass type of storm.

Warm-front thunderstorms are usually less violent than other types. Vertical air currents are not as pronounced, and the main action takes place aloft. Characteristic clouds for this type of thunderstorm are usually hidden by lower warm-front cloud types.

Many thunderstorms in summer occur along occluded fronts. Forces necessary for this type of storm are produced by the frontal uplifting of warm air, similar to the cold-front type of thunderstorm.

Thunderstorms may be produced over hilly and mountainous country by orographic uplifting. Rough terrain causes vertical turbulence, and moist air is forced rapidly upward as it rises over slopes. These ascending air currents free large sources of energy, and thunderstorms result. Another type of orographic storm occurs when moist air flows inland over seacoasts and ascends over sloping land.

In the beginning, every thunderstorm is a cumulus cloud. The actual development of a cumulus cloud into the complete cycle of a thunderstorm depends upon its environment. Warm, moist air flows into the cloud, carried aloft by a strong updraft. The bulging, mushrooming top of the cloud is an indication of this. As the upward motion continues, air flows into the sides of the cloud. A large amount of free water is liberated which, in time, becomes too heavy to be supported by the updraft and begins to fall. This falling water soon starts a downdraft in part of the cloud region. This downdraft of cool air reaches the ground and is the cause of a drop in temperature as the thunderstorm approaches. The downdraft eventually cuts off sources of the updraft and removes the ability of the warm

103

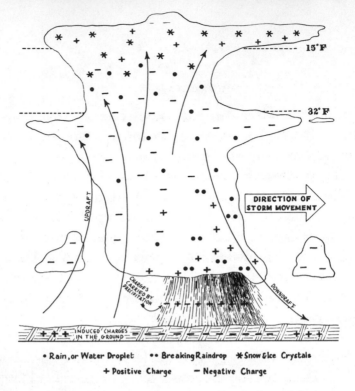

15° F

32° F

DIRECTION OF
STORM MOVEMENT

UPDRAFT

CHARGES
CARRIED BY
PRECIPITATION

DOWNDRAFT

INDUCED CHARGES
IN THE GROUND

• Rain, or Water Droplet   •• Breaking Raindrop   ✳ Snow & Ice Crystals
+ Positive Charge   — Negative Charge

Fig. 28   Cross section of typical thunderstorm.

moist air to enter the cloud. The thunderstorm has thus lost its source of energy and dissipates. Figure 28 shows a thunderstorm in its mature stage.

Thunderstorm lightning strokes are actually huge sparks jumping between positively and negatively charged areas in the cloud. Or lightning may occur between positive charges in the cloud and negative ground surfaces under it. The actual theory of the cause of these electrical charges is quite involved, but it is believed they result from the splitting apart of raindrops due to violent wind turbulence.

Hail: Raindrops, falling in a thunderstorm, may begin at high levels in the cloud as ice crystals. As they drop and melt, they unite with other water droplets and fall to the ground as raindrops. But sometimes, an ascending air current may carry the drops aloft again before they fall out of the cloud. When this occurs, the drops freeze. They may then fall, collect more water as they descend and possibly be blown

Fig. 29   Enlarged cross section through hail stone showing concentric layers. (*Photo by Laird-Lynott*)

upward a second time. This process may be repeated several times until the now relatively heavy ice balls fall to the ground as hailstones. Figure 29 shows a cross section of such a hailstone. Several layers of ice deposit may be seen.

Tornadoes: The most intense of all air movements is the tornado, a violent, funnel-shaped whirl a few hundred yards in diameter. Everyone is familiar with the destruction wrought by these storms. They are hard to forecast but occur only in regions of violent thunderstorm activity.

Hurricanes: A weather phenomenon of the autumn season in the United States is the hurricane. Hurricanes are similar in many respects to lows, but are smaller in diameter and more intense. They are accompanied by heavy rainfall and strong winds.

Fig. 30 Tornado. In the final photograph, the whirling funnel cloud has reached the ground and destruction has begun.

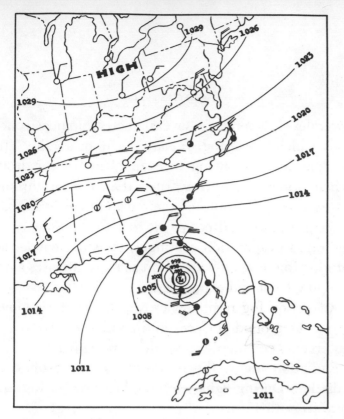

Fig. 31 Hurricane centered over Florida.

Hurricanes approach southeastern or southwestern United States from tropical waters. Their movement is slow and sometimes erratic. When a hurricane moves over land, its source of moisture and energy is cut off and it begins to behave like an ordinary low. Reports from ships, airplanes and seacoast stations furnish the forecaster with information on development and movement of hurricanes.

Fog: The process by which fog is formed is similar to that involved in cloud formation but on a much lower level. There are several meteorological conditions which cause fog. It may occur in a rainy area or along a front, owing to evaporation of raindrops. When water drops are warmer than the air through which they fall, some of their water will evaporate, causing unsaturated cooler air to saturate quickly. As this rapid evaporation continues, moisture condenses, forming fog. Fog may also form as moist air rises along a sloping front and condenses.

Advection fog results when warm, moist air moves over cold ground surfaces and condenses. Land and sea breezes commonly cause this type of fog.

Radiation fog is the result of surface cooling by radiation. During calm, clear nights, ground fog may form from this cause.

Cold Waves: A sudden push of cold, polar air, spreading rapidly southward from Canada, sometimes causes a cold wave. This is a mass of cold, dry air which has left its source region over the snow-covered areas of Alaska and Canada.

Usually an energetic and rapidly moving low is followed by a big high, a cold air mass. Temperatures drop radically and in a short time. The forecaster, noting advance of the cold air, must determine whether precipitation accompanying the preceding low will be in the form of rain or snow. The barometer rises rapidly with advance of a cold wave.

During summer months, wind movement in the United States is slower than in winter, and lows, highs and air masses move across the country at a slower rate. Weather sometimes seems to stagnate. Frequently, a high-pressure area will stall over the southeastern states, while a mass of warm air literally hangs over the central areas. This causes southerly winds to flow and a heat wave follows. It is sometimes difficult to forecast breakup of this condition.

In covering thus briefly the high points of forecasting weather, we hope the reader will bear in mind the need for weather map study as the one real aid in this pursuit. Cause, effect and results are prime requisites for accuracy in weather forecasting.

4

Instruments

The amateur meteorologist can go about as far as he wants to in the field of instrumentation. While it is gratifying to own shiny, expensive instruments and maintain an observatory equal to those operated by professional services, it is even more satisfying to build weather instruments according to your own taste and ability, from the plainest weather vane to the latest electronic device.

The following pages describe a few simple, reliable weather instruments which will add to your enjoyment of the study of weather. These instruments can be

Fig. 32 Instrument shelter with louvered sides and door.

constructed with common wood- and metal-working hand tools; no elaborate lathes, milling machines, et cetera, are required. Dimensions are not given in most cases. Size is up to the builder, who may want to use materials he already has on hand. When dimensions are shown, they may be changed if the builder uses the same ratios throughout the construction.

We believe that once you build any or all of the instruments described here, you will want to keep on constructing weather devices, possibly along lines you yourself may develop. Or you may want to buy fine factory-built instruments, once you have learned some of the basic principles of instrument construction.

Instrument Shelter for Exposure of Thermometers

As explained previously, a thermometer should be

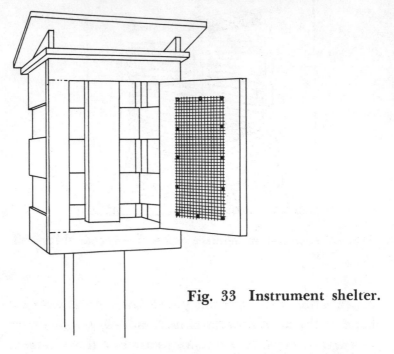

Fig. 33 Instrument shelter.

exposed to good air circulation, yet be protected from direct rays of the sun. Many instrument shelters have louvered sides, like the one shown in Figure 32. However, this type of shelter requires mortising tools plus considerable skill in its use.

The shelter shown in Figure 33 has slatted sides and is much easier to construct. Figure 33 shows how four pieces of wood are fitted together to form a door frame. If you plan to expose a single thermometer, the door frame should be about 18 in. high and 1 ft. wide. The door is similarly constructed. Be sure to use proper dimensions, so the door will fit snugly inside its frame. Tack coarse screen wire or hardware cloth inside the door opening. Attach door to frame

112

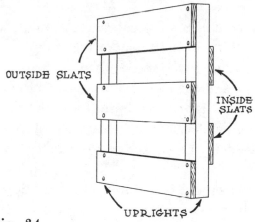

OUTSIDE SLATS

INSIDE SLATS

Fig. 34

UPRIGHTS

DETAIL OF WALL CONSTRUCTION —

with small hinges. If you're going to want to lock the door, add a small hasp and padlock.

For a small shelter, the four uprights, which constitute the corner posts of the shelter, may be made of sections of 2 in.-by-2 in. wood, 18 in. long. Use wood about 3/8 in. thick and 4 in. wide for the inside and outside slats. How these slats are fitted together to form the walls of the shelter is shown in Figure 34. The bottom of the shelter can be a square of plywood, with holes drilled to help maintain air circulation.

To protect instruments in the shelter from vertical sun rays, a double roof is advisable. But be sure to allow for free air circulation between the two roofs. The top roof should slant, and overhang the bottom

113

roof. To accomplish this, cut two slanting pieces of wood and nail them to the under roof from the underside. The under roof should then be nailed to the shelter sides, and the top roof fastened to the slanting pieces. Plywood is good material for both roofs.

The thermometer may be mounted on an upright board, placed in the center of the shelter, as shown in Figure 33.

The shelter should be painted white, inside and out, because white best reflects the sun's rays. Bolt the shelter to a post which is set in the ground. The shelter should be 5 ft. above the ground, mounted over sod with its door facing north. It should be placed away from buildings to allow free air circulation.

Some of the larger instrument shelters house maximum and minimum thermometers, psychrometric equipment (ventilated wet and dry bulb thermometers), a thermograph for making a continuous record

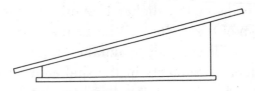

Fig. 35 **Top roof member of shelter should have a three or four inch overhang.**

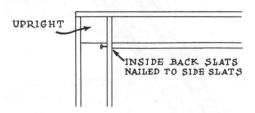

Fig. 36 Detail of shelter construction.

of day-to-day temperature and sometimes a hygro-graph for recording humidity.

Psychrometer

As explained previously, a psychrometer consists of two thermometers, mounted side-by-side and exposed to the air. The bulb of one thermometer is covered with a piece of thin, wet muslin. This thermometer is known as the wet bulb thermometer. In order to determine accurately the dew point and relative humidity from readings of the wet and dry bulb thermometers, they must be well ventilated. One of the simplest ways to do this is to mount the two thermometers on the same support and whirl, or "sling" them; hence, the term "sling psychrometer."

Get two good thermometers, 8 to 10 in. long, and cut the lower end of their back mountings away, as shown in Figure 37. If the backs are of wood, it is

115

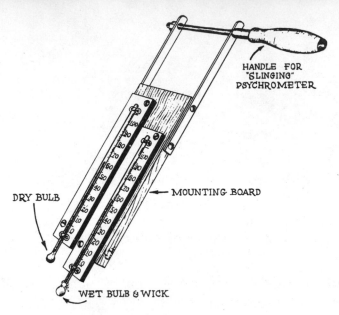

HANDLE FOR
"SLINGING"
PSYCHROMETER

DRY BULB

MOUNTING BOARD

WET BULB & WICK

Fig. 37   Sling psychrometer.

easy to remove the thermometer tubes from their mountings by removing the small straps, which are usually fastened on with small nails or screws. If your thermometers have a metal back, however, the straps may be riveted on, in which case you will have to drill them out with a metal drill. After the backs are cut away (if they are metal, you will need a hacksaw for this), re-fasten the thermometers to their mountings, using the same straps and small screws and nuts. Use care in handling the thermometer tubes, and be sure to return the tubes to the same backs.

Some of the best grade thermometers are obtainable with the bulb end of the thermometer already extending below the back, although these are more expensive than the variety shown here. As a rule, you

116

get what you pay for in thermometers, so buy the best you can afford.

Mount the two thermometers on a board (1/4 in. or 3/8 in. plywood), one about 1 in. lower than the other, as shown in Figure 37. This will assure good ventilation of the wet bulb, and likewise prevent the wet wick from having any effect on the dry bulb thermometer.

On each side of the upper end of this board, attach two strips, preferably brass stock 1/8 in. thick and as wide as the thickness of the board you use. These strips should extend several inches beyond the board, as shown in Figure 37. The handle is an ordinary file handle, bought in a hardware store; or you may whittle one out of a piece of wood if you desire. Drill a hole through the handle, large enough in diameter to accommodate a long bolt which extends through the brass strips.

Fig. 38   MUSLIN DISK
                             FOR
                           WET BULB

Figure 38 shows the cloth or wick for covering the wet bulb. It is a disk, cut from muslin, which should

117

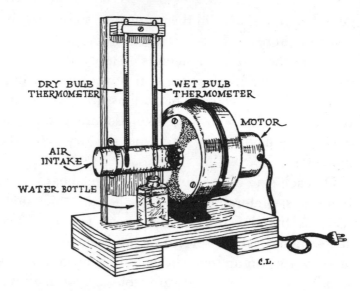

Fig. 39 Motor-driven psychrometer.

be well-washed before using. For best results, wash the muslin with soap and distilled water and then thoroughly rinse out the soap. The disk should have a white cotton thread run through it, as shown, so it can be pulled tight around the thermometer bulb. To use, dip the end of the wet bulb thermometer, with its muslin covering, in a container of distilled water.

Another type of psychrometer is shown in Figure 39. In this type, the thermometers extend into a tube through which air is drawn by an electrically driven blower. In this particular instrument, the ventilation

118

tube is made of plastic, although metal may be used. Also the thermometers have no backs and their scales are printed directly on the glass tube. Thermometers with backs may be used, however, with their backs cut away, as in the sling psychrometer. Thermometers and ventilation tube are supported by a vertical board which is mounted on a baseboard. The motor and blower are also mounted on this baseboard. The blower air outlet is mounted downward and the air exhausts through a hole in the baseboard. The wet bulb is kept moist by a long wick which extends downward into a bottle of distilled water.

There are other types of psychrometers. One has its wet and dry bulb thermometers mounted on a base in an instrument shelter, with a hand crank extending outside the shelter. The observer spins the crank and the psychrometer whirls, driven by a gear arrangement connected with the crank. In another, a hand-driven crank blows air across the thermometer bulbs. The important thing is an adequate air stream, with velocity of at least 15 ft. per second.

In all cases, the wick or wet bulb covering on a psychrometer should be clean. It is a good idea to change the wick once a week or oftener. Some instrument manufacturers furnish prepared wicks for wet bulb thermometers. It is also possible to buy muslin in tubular form, which may be cut off at the correct length

119

and tied around the thermometer bulb. This type of especially prepared muslin is probably the best kind to use for your psychrometer.

The observing section of this book has already explained how psychrometer readings are used to figure dew point and relative humidity.

Nephoscope

A nephoscope is used to determine speed and direction of clouds. Sometimes it consists of an elevated grid, through which clouds are observed. Another type uses a flat mirror, in which speed and direction of clouds are determined by watching cloud reflections. The nephoscope described here is of the latter type, and is probably the most commonly used.

A mirror of about 6 in. diameter is a good size to use. Obtain a glass disk (window glass will do) and paint it black on one side. A black mirror of this type is excellent for observing clouds.

The base of the nephoscope consists of a disk of 3/4 in. plywood, about 10 in. in diameter. Projecting from this base are three short lengths of wood, extending out about 1 in. and fastened to the underside of the plywood disk with small nails or screws. These three sections of wood are arranged at equal distances apart around the disk, as shown in Figure 40. Extend-

120

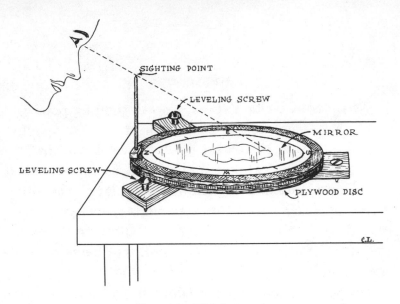

Fig. 40 Nephoscope.

ing through these wood sections are three wood-leveling screws. They should be 1 in. or more in length. Drill small "starting holes" in the wood sections before turning in the screws, so as not to split the wood. The pointed end of the screws should be rounded off a bit with a file so they won't mar the table which supports the nephoscope.

Glue the mirror, painted side down, to the top side of the plywood disk. Be sure to center it on the disk. Put a small dot of white paint in the exact center of the mirror. Also glue a circle of paper around the mirror, flat on the plywood surface. The circle may be graduated in degrees (0 to 360), or marked in the eight directions, N, NW, W, et cetera, and is used for determining cloud direction.

121

To determine cloud speed, a small sighting point is necessary. This consists of a piece of 1/4 in. dowel, glued in a hole in a small block of wood. Height of this point is critical and is contained in the formula for determining cloud speed described later. You will want several lengths, but you might start with one with its tip at a height, above the bottom surface of the mirror, which is equal to the radius of the mirror—for example, 3 in., if you use a 6 in. mirror.

Set the nephoscope on a table; or you can build a special pedestal for it. The important thing is to be sure the mirror sets level. To accomplish this, place a small spirit level on the mirror surface and adjust two of the leveling screws until the mirror is level. Also important is that the nephoscope be placed so the "south" direction on the paper scale actually points north. Use a compass to be exact.

To determine cloud direction, place the sighting point in a position around the mirror so that a cloud image appears at the dot in the center of the mirror. Watch the movement of this image, keeping it in line with the sighting point. The direction in which the cloud is moving can be determined by observing the point on the graduated scale where the image passes off the mirror. With the nephoscope oriented in the manner described above (with north on the paper scale actually pointing south), the direction from which the cloud is moving will correspond to the direction on the scale graduation toward which the cloud image moves.

Getting the cloud speed is somewhat more difficult. It depends for accuracy on a knowledge of cloud height above the ground. You should use a stop watch to determine the time it takes the cloud image to travel from the center of the mirror to its edge. After sighting the cloud image in the manner shown above, start the watch the instant you have the image located at the center of the mirror and stop it when the image reaches the edge. The formula for cloud speed is:

$$\text{Speed} = \frac{\text{Cloud height} \times \text{mirror radius}}{\text{Height of pointer} \times \text{time}}$$

If the sighting point you use is the same length as the mirror radius, the formula can be shortened to:

$$\text{Speed} = \frac{\text{Cloud height}}{\text{Time}}$$

If you use cloud height in feet and time in seconds, the answer, of course, is in feet-per-second. You may want to convert this to miles-per-hour.

Determination of cloud height is not always easy, although observers can become quite adept at judging this distance by eye observation alone. Ceiling balloons, ceiling lights and the newer automatic ceilometers are valuable aids in determining cloud elevation but are too elaborate and expensive for most weather hobbyists. Until you become good at judging cloud height, you might get that information from a nearby Weather Bureau office.

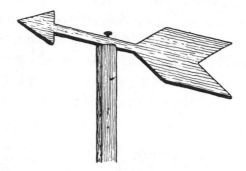

Fig. 41 A simple wind vane.

Wind Vane

One of the oldest weather instruments is the wind vane or weather vane. It can be very simple to build, or it may be developed into a complicated device that indicates or records wind direction remotely.

The best wind vanes have good bearings, solid mechanical construction and durability. But as a starter, you might whittle a vane out of wood, something like the one shown in Figure 41. After you have finished shaping it, find the balance point between the tail and

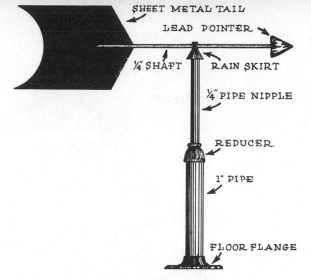

SHEET METAL TAIL

LEAD POINTER

¼" SHAFT   RAIN SKIRT

¼" PIPE NIPPLE

REDUCER

1" PIPE

FLOOR FLANGE

Fig. 42 All metal wind vane.

pointer end and drill a small hole. A large nail can serve as the bearing shaft, and you can mount the vane on top of a stick or post. Use a washer between the vane and its support to reduce the turning friction.

A better vane is the one shown in Figure 42. It is constructed entirely of metal, from parts and materials easily obtainable. Dimensions are given, but they do not necessarily need to be followed. Actually, wind vanes lend themselves to a variety of sizes and patterns. The tail in particular can have almost any shape you desire.

The tail in this vane may be cut from sheet aluminum, galvanized iron or other sheet metal. It is 8 in. long and 6 in. high. The horizontal shaft, with tail on one end and pointer (counterweight) on the other, is 12 in. long and has a diameter of 1/4 in. The counter-

125

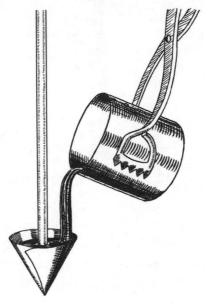

Fig. 43 Pouring lead into mold forming wind vane pointer

weight is made by pouring hot lead into a form made of sheet metal shaped into a cone (Figure 43). Or you can saw a piece of lead into an arrowhead shape. If the pointer is made by the first method, the end of the shaft should be inserted in the form before pouring in the hot lead. The weight of the pointer is not too important. The way to balance it with the tail will be given later.

Figure 44 shows one method of constructing the vane

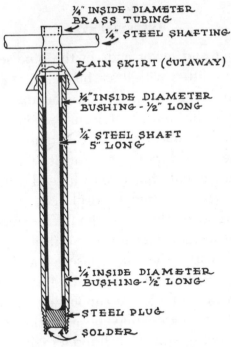

¼" INSIDE DIAMETER
BRASS TUBING
¼" STEEL SHAFTING

RAIN SKIRT (CUTAWAY)

¼"INSIDE DIAMETER
BUSHING - ½" LONG

¼" STEEL SHAFT
5" LONG

¼" INSIDE DIAMETER
BUSHING-½" LONG

STEEL PLUG

SOLDER

Fig. 44 Wind vane bearing.

bearing. A 5 in. length of 1/4 in. metal pipe forms the bearing housing. Its lower end is threaded with standard pipe threads. For this housing, you may use a standard 1/4 in. pipe nipple (6 in. long). Since pipe nipples are threaded on both ends, cut off 1 in. of one threaded end with a hacksaw. The remaining 5 in. will be about the right length. A pipe of this size actually has an inside diameter of about 3/8 in., which allows ample room for the vertical vane spindle and its bearings.

The upper and lower ends of the pipe section just described are fitted with brass bushings, 1/4 in. inside diameter and 1/2 in. in length. You may use brass tubing 1/4 in. inside diameter and 3/8 in. outside diameter, but you may have to do some filing to get them in the pipe, forming a tight fit. The lower end of the pipe section should be plugged with a piece of 3/8 in. steel shafting or drill rod, 1/2 in. long. The upper end of this plug should be smooth, as it forms the bearing surface for the vertical vane spindle. Heat the pipe after the plug is inserted and use a little solder to seal it. This will make it oil-tight.

The vertical vane spindle supporting the vane, and upon which it rotates, may be a section of 1/4 in. shafting; or better still, of drill rod 5 in. in length. The lower end should be rounded off with a file, then smoothed with a crocus cloth. Or it may be rounded with a lathe if you have access to one. The rotating vane is then supported by the rounded end of this steel spindle resting on the steel plug, forming an almost frictionless bearing.

A section of 1/4 in. inside diameter brass tubing is used to fasten the horizontal vane shaft to the top of the steel spindle. The outside diameter of this section of tubing is not critical. It should be about 1 in. long. Drill a 1/4 in. hole perpendicularly through this section near one end. Through this hole goes the vane shaft. Before inserting it, split the shaft on the end opposite the arrow with a hacksaw, making a cut about 3 in. long. After introducing the shaft through the hole, the tail is slipped into the cut and soldered, riveted, or fastened with small bolts.

The vertical spindle and horizontal shaft are now ready to be soldered into the 1 in. length of brass tubing. But first assemble them, pushing the vane shaft back and forth until it balances. The parts should fit snugly, so they will remain that way while you heat the brass tubing and apply solder.

A small cone, or "rain skirt," may be soldered to the brass tubing as shown in Figure 44. The purpose of this skirt is to keep rain out of the vane bearing.

You may use a standard reducer coupling at the lower end of the pipe to join it to a 1 in. or larger pipe which acts as the vane support. This may be of any reasonable length. A wind vane and anemometer support may be built with standard pipe and fittings, as shown in Figure 45. This will make a very durable and professional-looking mast for your wind instruments. The lower end of the pipe support can be screwed into a standard floor flange for mounting on a roof.

Before putting the vane into use, a little light machine oil should be poured into the 5 in. length of pipe forming the vane bearing. The bearing should be cleaned out and re-oiled about twice a year.

Fig. 45 Wind vane and anemometer on pipe-fitting support.

Anemometer

Probably the most common instrument for determining wind speed is the cup anemometer. This instrument consists of three or four hollow cups or cones, mounted on horizontal arms and supported by a vertical shaft. Air moving past the cups rotates the assembly, and the speed of this rotation shows the wind speed.

130

The cup anemometer was invented by a man named Robinson, who assumed that speed of rotation in relation to wind movement was constant for all anemometers, regardless of size of the cups and length of the cup arms. Not only has this theory been proven wrong, but it has also been discovered that the relation of wind movement to anemometer rotation is not constant at all wind speeds, even with the same anemometer. Mathematical formulae have been used to calibrate anemometers, and instrument makers resort to wind tunnels for establishing accuracy of their products. Such elaborate methods are beyond the scope of most amateur meteorologists. A simpler method of calibration can be used for the anemometer described here.

In some anemometers, the speed of the vertical shaft is reduced by gears, with an electrical contact made each time the shaft rotates a certain number of times —for example, 25. A simple electrical circuit, consisting of buzzer, battery and switch, is wired in series with the anemometer contacts. When the switch is turned on, the buzzer sounds each time the anemometer cups rotate 25 times. If the dimensions of the cup assembly are such that the assembly rotates 1,500 times for each mile of wind, each buzz indicates that 1/60 mile of wind has passed. In other words, the number of buzzes in one minute indicates the wind speed in miles-per-hour. However, the indicated ve-

131

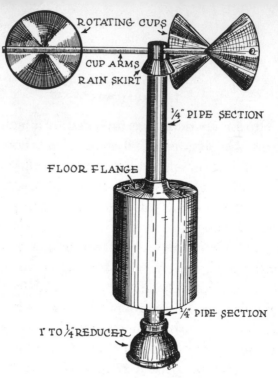

Labels on figure:
ROTATING CUPS
CUP ARMS
RAIN SKIRT
¼" PIPE SECTION
FLOOR FLANGE
¼" PIPE SECTION
1" TO ¼" REDUCER

Fig. 46   Anemometer.

locity is not always correct at all speeds, and corrections are usually applied at very low and very high velocities.

The three cones used in the anemometer described here are made of thin copper and have a diameter of 2 in. at the open end. The angle of the cone should be about 90 degrees. Each of the cones is soldered on one end of a 4 in. section of 1/8 in. round shafting, as shown in Figure 46. The vertical shaft should have a diameter of at least 1/8 in., but this dimension may vary, depending on the gears obtainable. The three cone arms are soldered into holes drilled an equal

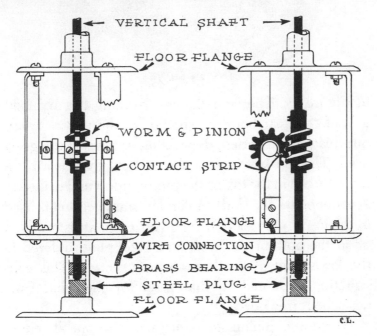

VERTICAL SHAFT

FLOOR FLANGE

WORM & PINION

CONTACT STRIP

FLOOR FLANGE

WIRE CONNECTION

BRASS BEARING

STEEL PLUG

FLOOR FLANGE

C.L.

Fig. 47 Front and side view of anemometer
mechanism.

distance apart in a section of round brass stock about
1/2 in. long. The vertical shaft is then soldered in a
hole drilled to accommodate it in the section of brass
stock so that the shaft is perpendicular to the cup
arms. A cone-shaped rain shield may be added to the
cup arm assembly (Figure 46).

Two sections of iron pipe, 3/8 in. inside diameter,
serve as a support for the anemometer. The upper
section should be 4 in. long; the lower, 2 in. to 4 in.
Two ordinary pipe floor flanges serve to separate
these pipe sections, held together with pieces of 1/8
in.-by-3/8 in. brass stock, bent and drilled as shown

133

in Figure 47. The floor flanges, forming top and bottom of the gear housing, should be about 3 in. apart, but this may be varied, depending on sizes of the gears used. The top bearing for the vertical shaft is a brass plug, forced in the top of the pipe support and drilled to accommodate the shaft. A similar brass bearing is used in the lower pipe section. The vertical shaft is rounded off at the bottom and rests on a steel plug soldered in the lower end of the bottom pipe section. This construction is similar to that used for the wind vane described previously.

Worm and pinion gears are used for speed reduction. They should have a ratio of about 1 to 25, although this, too, may be varied. The worm gear is mounted on the vertical shaft and the pinion gear is supported by a short horizontal shaft turning in bearings made of two sections of 3/8 in.-by-1/8 in. brass stock, which are bolted to the floor flange forming the bottom of the gear housing. Two collars are mounted on the ends of the shaft carrying the pinion shaft.

Gears may be of the type used in toy construction sets, such as Erector. Or you may get them from other sources, such as an old electric clock. A thin brass strip mounted on a block of insulating material, such as fiber, makes contact with the setscrew on one of the collars, so that a circuit is closed once for each revolu-

134

tion of the pinion gear. The fiber block is bolted to one of the upright sections of brass stock forming the pinion bearing. The brass strip must be insulated from the rest of the anemometer. A sheet metal cylindrical cover slips over the gear housing, protecting the gears from rain.

To hook up the anemometer, run a wire from the brass strip to one terminal of a battery consisting of two dry cells. A wire from the opposite terminal of the battery goes to a switch, then to one side of an ordinary buzzer. Run another wire from the other terminal of the buzzer to the body or ground side of the anemometer (see Figure 47). When contact is made in the anemometer, the buzzer will sound. The wires running to the anemometer may be of any reasonable length, although you may have to add another dry cell or two if they are very long. Use No. 16 wire or larger.

To calibrate the anemometer, mount it on a stick or section of pipe so it can be held outside of an automobile window and somewhat higher than the top of the car. Have someone drive the car at a constant speed, and find the time in minutes and seconds that it takes the anemometer to contact the buzzer the number of times represented by that speed. Thus, if the speed is 10 miles per hour, the time required is that for 10 buzzes; if it is 15 miles per hour, the time for 15 buzzes is measured; 25 buzzes for 25 miles per hour, and so forth. Now turn the car around and repeat this procedure in the opposite direction. Use the average time obtained from driving in both directions. This is to compensate for (average out) the natural wind velocity at the time. If you can do this calibrating on a calm day, the results will be more accurate, and they can be further improved by increasing the number of test runs in opposite directions. Use the average for all calibration runs.

The anemometer may not respond to very high and very low winds in quite the same way. For example, at 40 miles per hour the number of buzzes in the unit time may be more or less than 40, indicating that a correction to high-speed readings is necessary. In fact, the best way to record the calibration is to try as many car speeds as possible and draw up a curve of the averages.

We have made no attempt to construct our anemometer so it operates in accordance with the example given at the beginning of this chapter. In other words, while a one-minute unit of time is convenient, it is not essential. In the calibration system described above, we know the automobile's speed. Thus the time required to produce the number of buzzes equal to the automobile's speed becomes the basic unit of time for our anemometer.

136

After it is calibrated, the anemometer may be mounted for use. If you care to mount it on a roof-top or post, screw the bottom pipe section into a floor flange as shown in Figure 47. Or you may use a reducer coupling as shown in Figure 46 and mount it on a pipe support. It may be mounted in combination with the wind vane as shown in Figure 45, using standard pipes and fittings for the support.

Mercurial Barometer

The most widely used method of measuring atmospheric pressure is to balance it against something constant—the weight of a column of liquid. The most convenient liquid has been found to be mercury. When this mercury is placed in a glass tube, sealed at one end and with its other end inserted in a container of the same liquid, we have what is known as a mercurial barometer. As the level of mercury in this tube rises and falls, the observer is able to follow progress of high- and low-pressure areas across his particular region.

In its basic form it is quite a simple piece of apparatus, both to build and operate. The one described here, while made with very little outlay of materials, has all the essentials of more expensive instruments.

First of all, you will have to obtain some mercury —about a pound of it. It should be clean and pure,

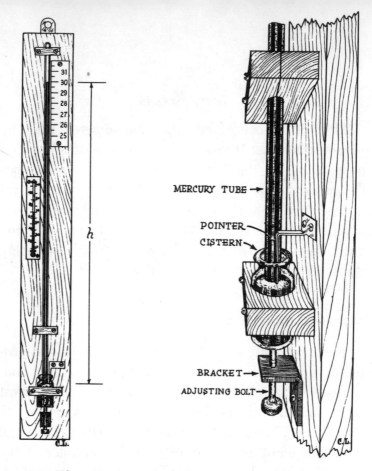

Fig. 48 Completed barometer (left).

Fig. 49 View of cistern and associated parts (right).

and may be purchased at most large drugstores.

The whole assembly is mounted on a support made of 3/4 in. pine or other straight-grained wood, about 40 1/2 in. long and 5 in. wide; or 1/2 in. plywood will do. This is shown in Figures 48 and 49. Make a hanger for the barometer by fastening a length of thin

138

strip metal, with a hole drilled in one end, to the back of the support. See Figure 50.

Fig. 50 Hanger for back of mounting board.

A section of glass tubing about 1/4 in. inside diameter and 35 in. long will serve as barometer tubing. Neon sign companies are a good source of glass tubing. The diameter of this glass tubing is not critical and does not affect the accuracy of the instrument. By using 1/4 in. inside diameter tubing, however, you won't need as much mercury as larger tubing requires.

Seal the glass tubing at one end by heating that end over a gas flame and slowly rotating it until it is completely closed. You can do this over the flame of a gas stove.

For the mercury container, or cistern, you may use a small glass bottle, such as a pill bottle, about 3 in. long and 1 in. inside diameter. These dimensions are not critical. The cistern is mounted in a hole cut in a wooden block about 3/4 in. thick and fastened to the wood support with long wood screws, as shown in Figure 49. The top of this block should be about 4 in. from the bottom of the barometer mounting board. The size of the hole in the block will depend, of course, on the outside diameter of the cistern bottle. It should be large enough so the bottle will fit snugly but still be able to slide vertically through it. The bottom of the cistern rests on a metal bolt threaded into an L-shaped metal support about 1 in. wide that can be made of 1/4 in. brass or other metal stock. This supporting bolt should have a wing or gnurled nut soldered on its lower end. A 1/4 in. brass bolt will serve very well and should be about 2 in. in length.

The vertical glass tube containing the column of mercury may be clamped to the mounting board by running it through two split blocks of wood drilled to a size to accommodate the outside diameter, as shown in Figures 49 and 51. A hole of the proper size to conform to the tubing should be drilled in a block cut of 3/4 in. wood. The blocks are then drilled for two long wood screws, which are used to fasten them to the mounting board. The distance between the mercury tube hole and the mounting board will depend on the size of the bottle you use for the cistern. The tube should be centered in the bottle. After drilling the

140

blocks, saw them in two across the tubing hole, as shown in Figure 51.

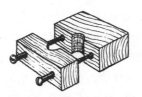

Fig. 51 Split block for fastening mercury tube to mounting board.

You will need a mercury level pointer shaped as shown in Figure 49. It may be made of thin sheet iron, but do not use galvanized metal, which contaminates mercury. Later we will fasten this pointer to the mounting board, with its point extending into the cistern, as shown in the drawing.

The height of the mercury in the column, i.e., barometric pressure, is determined by fastening a section of ruler alongside the tube. It should be at least 7 in. long. Barometric pressure is almost always expressed in inches and 10ths, or in millibars. For our purpose, a scale marked in inches and 10ths will be most practical. Conversion from inches to millibars or vice versa is simple. You may use a section of ready-made ruler, or you can mark off inches and 10ths on a strip of wood or even paper.

141

If you live near sea level, where the average pressure is 29.92, the inch marks on the ruler should be numbered as shown in Figure 48. At higher altitudes, there are two procedures possible. The scale may be marked to range somewhat above and below the average pressure for that altitude (1,000 feet, 28.86 in.; 2,000, 27.82; 3,000, 26.82; 4,000, 25.84; 5,000, 24.90; 6,000, 23.98; 7,000, 23.09; 8,000, 22.22). Or the pressure, reduced to sea level, may be read directly by shortening the entire instrument to correspond to the difference between your altitude and sea level. The important thing to remember, in building a barometer such as this, is to have each particular division on the scale the correct distance from the tip of the metal point which dips into the cistern. For example, the 30 in. division must be exactly 30 in. above the tip of the metal pointer. This is shown as height, or "h," in Figure 48.

In assembling the barometer, put about 1/2 in. of the mercury in the cistern. Mercury is slippery, so be sure to do your pouring over a large basin or enamel vessel to catch any that spills. Next, invert the glass tube so its open end is upward. You can use a funnel with a very small opening to fill the tube with mercury. Probably the best is a simple cone made with a piece of paper, such as heavy bond. Now carefully pour the mercury through the funnel into the glass tube, which should be held at an angle so the mercury does not plop down against the sealed end and break the tube. Pour it slowly, and tap the tube while filling it to drive out air bubbles. In the filling of some barometer tubes, the tube is heated, section by section, as the mercury is poured in. This tends to drive out moisture and fine air bubbles, but this is only done in the interest of greater accuracy and does not need to be followed in our barometer. If you do heat it, do so in open air because highly poisonous mercury vapor fumes are driven off by the heating.

When the tube is completely filled, draw a strip of heavy rubber, about 1/2 in. wide and 8 in. long, tightly over the open end of the tube. A piece cut from an old automobile innertube will do very well (see Figure 52). Slowly invert the tube and lower the open end into the cistern, still holding the rubber strip tight to prevent escape of the mercury. When the end of the mercury-filled tube is well below the mercury level in the cistern, pull out the rubber strip. The mercury will drop in the tube until its weight balances the atmospheric pressure, forming a vacuum at the top of the tube.

You can now put the cistern in its support block and clamp the tube to the mounting board. The bottom end of the vertical mercury tube should be at least 1/16 in. above the inside bottom of the cistern. Have the split

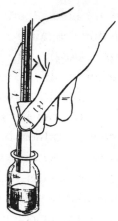

Fig. 52 Manner of inserting mercury tube into cistern.

blocks supporting the tube tight enough so the tube won't slip down. It isn't a bad idea to line the split hole in the blocks with rubber to help prevent slipping and to avoid breaking the tube when the blocks are tightened.

The cistern should be about 3/4 full of mercury. To achieve this level, you may have to remove a little of the mercury from the cistern with a small non-metallic spoon or paper scoop.

Fasten the pointer to the mounting board, with its tip at about the level of the mercury surface. Now also is the time to mount the ruler, marked in inches and tenths. Again a word of caution about accuracy. It

144

should be mounted at exactly the proper height above the tip of the pointer.

To read the barometer, the adjusting screw or bolt which supports the cistern is turned until the metal point, which remains stationary, rests on top of the mercury in the cistern. The height of the mercury (barometer reading) is then read off the ruler. When atmospheric pressure rises, mercury will be high in the barometer tube and lower in the cistern. When pressure drops, the opposite is true.

The temperature of the air surrounding the barometer will affect its readings, owing to expansion and contraction of the mercury. For accurate pressure determination, the barometer should be corrected for air temperature. A thermometer may be mounted on the barometer, as shown in Figure 48.

Correction of Mercurial Barometer for Temperature

Attached Thermometer Reading F.	24	25	26	27	28	29	30	31
				SUBTRACT				
40	.025	.026	.027	.028	.029	.030	.031	.032
41	.027	.028	.029	.030	.031	.033	.034	.035
42	.029	.030	.032	.033	.034	.035	.036	.038
43	.031	.033	.034	.035	.036	.038	.039	.040
44	.033	.035	.036	.038	.039	.040	.042	.043
45	.036	.037	.039	.040	.042	.043	.045	.046
46	.038	.039	.041	.043	.044	.046	.047	.049
47	.040	.042	.043	.045	.047	.048	.050	.052
48	.042	.044	.046	.047	.049	.051	.053	.054
49	.044	.046	.048	.050	.052	.054	.055	.057
50	.046	.048	.050	.052	.054	.056	.058	.060
51	.049	.051	.053	.055	.057	.059	.061	.063
52	.051	.053	.055	.057	.059	.061	.064	.066
53	.053	.055	.057	.060	.062	.064	.066	.068
54	.055	.057	.060	.062	.064	.067	.069	.071
55	.057	.060	.062	.064	.067	.069	.072	.074
56	.060	.062	.064	.067	.069	.072	.074	.077
57	.062	.064	.067	.069	.072	.075	.077	.080
58	.064	.066	.069	.072	.074	.077	.080	.082
59	.066	.069	.072	.074	.077	.080	.083	.085
60	.068	.071	.074	.077	.080	.082	.085	.088
61	.070	.073	.076	.079	.082	.085	.088	.091
62	.073	.076	.079	.082	.085	.088	.091	.094
63	.075	.078	.081	.084	.087	.090	.093	.096
64	.077	.080	.083	.086	.090	.093	.096	.099
65	.079	.082	.086	.089	.092	.095	.099	.102
66	.081	.085	.088	.091	.095	.098	.101	.105
67	.083	.087	.090	.094	.097	.101	.104	.108
68	.085	.089	.093	.096	.100	.103	.107	.110
69	.088	.091	.095	.099	.102	.106	.110	.113
70	.090	.094	.097	.101	.105	.109	.112	.116
71	.092	.096	.100	.103	.107	.111	.115	.119
72	.094	.098	.102	.106	.110	.114	.118	.122
73	.096	.100	.104	.108	.112	.116	.120	.124
74	.098	.103	.107	.111	.115	.119	.123	.127

146

Correction of Mercurial Barometer for Temperature

Attached Thermometer Reading F.	Observed reading of barometer in inches							
	24	25	26	27	28	29	30	31
				SUBTRACT				
75	.101	.105	.109	.113	.117	.122	.126	.130
76	.103	.107	.111	.116	.120	.124	.128	.133
77	.105	.109	.114	.118	.122	.127	.131	.136
78	.107	.112	.116	.120	.125	.129	.134	.138
79	.109	.114	.118	.123	.127	.132	.137	.141
80	.111	.116	.121	.125	.130	.135	.139	.144
81	.114	.118	.123	.128	.132	.137	.142	.147
82	.116	.121	.125	.130	.135	.140	.145	.149
83	.118	.123	.128	.133	.138	.142	.147	.152
84	.120	.125	.130	.135	.140	.145	.150	.155
85	.122	.127	.132	.137	.143	.148	.153	.158
86	.124	.130	.135	.140	.145	.150	.155	.161
87	.126	.132	.137	.142	.148	.153	.158	.163
88	.129	.134	.139	.145	.150	.155	.161	.166
89	.131	.136	.142	.147	.153	.158	.164	.169
90	.133	.138	.144	.150	.155	.161	.166	.172
91	.135	.141	.146	.152	.158	.163	.169	.175
92	.137	.143	.149	.154	.160	.166	.172	.177
93	.139	.145	.151	.157	.163	.168	.174	.180
94	.142	.147	.153	.159	.165	.171	.177	.183
95	.144	.150	.156	.162	.168	.174	.180	.186
96	.146	.152	.158	.164	.170	.176	.182	.188
97	.148	.154	.160	.167	.173	.179	.185	.191
98	.150	.156	.163	.169	.175	.181	.188	.194
99	.152	.159	.165	.171	.178	.184	.190	.197
100	.154	.161	.167	.174	.180	.187	.193	.200

Rain Gage

As touched on in the section on observing, a rain gage should be of the multiplying type, so that rainfall may be accurately measured. The standard rain gage of the Weather Bureau has a funnel with an 8 in. diameter, with a rim about 2 in. high around the mouth of this funnel to prevent water from splashing off the funnel, thereby rendering the measurement inaccurate. Precipitation flows into a measuring tube with 1/10 the area of the mouth of the funnel and is then measured by inserting a thin ruler, divided into inches and tenths, into the tube to determine the height of the water. The result is divided by 10 to get the actual amount of rainfall. Thus 10 in. of water in the rain gage means 1 in. of rain has fallen.

A reasonably accurate rain gage can be built as shown in Figures 53 and 54. The measuring tube in this rain gage has an inside diameter of 2 in. and is 10 in. in length. It may be constructed from standard 2 in. inside diameter brass tubing, or it can be made of sheet metal. A disk of metal with a diameter equal to the outside diameter of the tube should be soldered on one end to form the bottom.

Fig. 53 Rain gage.

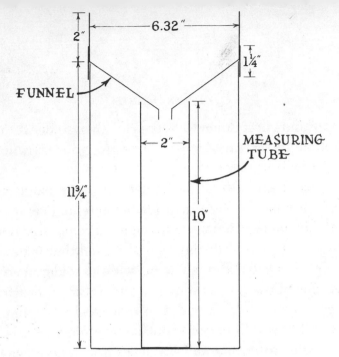

Fig. 54 Dimensions of rain gage.

The funnel should have a diameter at the mouth or large end of 6.32 in., topped by a rim 2 in. high with the same inside diameter. Since the upper edge of the rim determines the amount of precipitation that falls into the gage, its diameter must be accurate. This rim may be made of a strip of sheet metal 2 in. wide and 19.85 in. long. About 1/2 in. more should be allowed for overlap for soldering. Better results could be obtained by having this rim turned on a lathe from brass stock. The top outside edge should be beveled at about a 45-degree angle to eliminate any flat surface from which rain might splash into the gage.

You may buy a funnel if you care to at a hardware

149

store and cut it down to fit the rim, then solder it to the bottom of the rim. Or you can make your own funnel out of sheet metal.

Like the mouth of the funnel, the outer container of the gage should have an inside diameter of 6.32 in. The one shown here is 11 3/4 in. high, although this height may be varied to fit the type of funnel that is used. A strip of sheet metal 1 1/4 in. wide is soldered to the outside of the rim, as shown in the drawing. It extends down about half its width so that the funnel and rim assembly will fit over the outside container.

A thin ruler, marked in inches and tenths, may be used to measure the water in the inside tube.

If you want a less elaborate gage, accurate results may still be obtained by using the same type of measuring tube and the outer container only. The container alone is exposed to the weather, and its contents are poured into the tube for measuring after each period of precipitation.

When the temperature is below freezing or expected to be below freezing, and there is a possibility of snow, the container only is exposed. The snow it catches is melted by bringing the container into a warm room. The liquid content may then be poured into the measuring tube and measured. Water freezing in the 2 in. tube will cause the tube to buckle or break open, so it's best to expose the outer container only in the winter months.

The gage may be mounted by using four stakes driven into the ground far enough apart so the gage fits into them snugly (Figure 53). The gage should be exposed far enough away from trees and buildings so they will offer no obstruction.

Index

a, weather symbol, 67
ABI, 61
Abilene, Tex.:
  station letters, 61
  station number, 61
ABQ, 62
Air mass:
  characteristics, 78-79
  origin:
    Arctic, 79
    Polar, 78
    superior, 79
    Tropical, 78
  symbols, 78-79
ALB, 62
Albany, N. Y.:
  station letters, 62
  station number, 62
Albuquerque, N. M.:
  station letters, 62
  station number, 62
Alpena, Mich.:
  station letters, 62
  station number, 62
Altimeter setting:
  how expressed, 80-81
  use, 81
Altocumulus clouds (*see* Clouds,
  altocumulus)
Altostratus clouds (*see* Clouds,
  altostratus)

AMA, 62
Amarillo, Tex.:
  station letters, 62
  station number, 62
Anemometer:
  building instructions, 130-137
  use, 30-31
Aneroid barometer, 34
APN, 62
ATL, 61
Atlanta, Ga.:
  station letters, 61
  station number, 61
Atmospheric pressure (*see* Barometric pressure)

Barograph, 34
Barometer, aneroid, 34
Barometer, mercurial, 34 (*see also*
  Barometric pressure *and*
  Mercurial barometer)
Barometric pressure:
  aneroid barometer, 34
  barograph, 34
  change, amount of, 87
  defined, 34
  forecasting:
    colder, 55
    fair, 54
    fair, continued, 54
    storms, 53

Barometric pressure (*cont.*):
forecasting, importance to, 37
highs:
how recognized, 86
origin of term, 86
how expressed, 34
instruments for determining, 33-34
lows:
how recognized, 86
origin of term, 86
paths of movement, 96-97
precipitation, 93-95
speed of movement, 97
mercurial barometer:
building instructions, 137-147
described, 34
temperature correction
(*table*), 146-147
millibars:
converting inches to millibars
(*table*), 35-36
defined, 34
sea-level pressure, 37
station pressure, 37
tendency (*code table*), 71
Washington weather map, 56
Beaufort table, 32
BHM, 61
Birmingham, Ala.:
station letters, 61
station number, 61
BNA, 62
BOI, 62
Boise, Idaho:
station letters, 62
station number, 62
BOS, 62
Boston, Mass.:
station letters, 62
station number, 62
BRO, 61
Brownsville, Tex.:
station letters, 61
station number, 61

CAA stations (*see* Radio range stations)
Cape Hatteras, N. C.:
station letters, 61
station number, 61
CAR, 62
Caribou, Maine:
station letters, 62
station number, 62
Casper, Wyo.:
station letters, 62
station number, 62
Ceilometer, 18
C_H, weather symbol, 67
Charleston, S. C.:
station letters, 61
station number, 61
Cheyenne, Wyo.:
station letters, 62
station number, 62
CHI, 62
Chicago, Ill.:
station letters, 62
station number, 62
CHS, 61
Cirrocumulus clouds (*see* Clouds, cirrocumulus)
Cirrostratus clouds (*see* Clouds, cirrostratus)
Cirrus clouds (*see* Clouds, cirrus)
Cirrusnothus clouds, 14
C_L, weather symbol, 66
Clinometer, 18
Clouds:
altocumulus:
abbreviated, 10
described, 47
height, 16-17
rain, when they indicate, 47-48
snow, when they indicate, 47-48
USWB photographs, 13, 14
virga, 47

Clouds (*cont.*):
altostratus:
abbreviated, 10
described, 48
height, 16-17
storms, when they indicate, 48
USWB photograph, 12
cirrocumulus:
abbreviated, 10
described, 14, 46
rain, when they indicate, 46-47
US Army photograph, 11
cirrostratus:
abbreviated, 10
described, 14, 47
fair, when they indicate, 47
rain, when they indicate, 47
warmer, when they indicate, 47
cirrus:
abbreviated, 10
described, 13-14, 46
fair, when they indicate, 46
height, 17
mackerel sky, 13
mare's-tails, 13
rain, when they indicate, 46
snow, when they indicate, 46
USWB photograph, 10
cirrusnothus, 14
code tables:
amount, 70
direction, 69
height, 70
types, 68
cumulonimbus:
abbreviated, 11
described, 16, 49-50
USWB photograph, 16
weather, type they indicate, 49-50
cumulus:
abbreviated, 11
described, 16

Clouds (*cont.*):
cumulus (*cont.*):
height, 17
photographs, 15, 17
thunderstorm development, 103-104
USWB photograph, 15
cumulus, fair weather:
described, 49
weather, kind they precede, 49
direction:
how to determine, 19
nephoscope, 19, 120-123
forecasting:
colder, 55
fair, 54
fair, continued, 54
storms, 53
warmer, 55
formation, 24, 91:
coalescence, 91
collision, 91
condensation, 91
condensation nuclei, 91
droplets, 91
super-cooling, 91
fractocumulus, abbreviated, 11
fractostratus, abbreviated, 11
height:
alto prefix, 17
ceilometer, 18
cirrus, 17
clinometer, 18
cumulus, 17
high altitude, 17
low altitude, 17
medium altitude, 14-15
middle clouds, 17
ways to determine, 18-19
manuscript map, entered on, 56
nimbostratus:
abbreviated, 11
described, 49

Clouds (*cont.*):
  nimbostratus (*cont.*):
    height, 16
    USWB photographs, 12, 15
    weather, kind they precede,
      49
  sky coverage:
    broken clouds, 20
    clear, 19
    how expressed, 19-20
    obscuration, 19
    overcast, 20
    partial obscuration, 19
    scattered clouds, 19
    USWB symbols, 19-20
  speed of travel:
    how to determine, 19
    nephoscope, 19, 120-123
  stratocumulus:
    abbreviated, 10-11
    described, 16, 48
    forecasting, significance to,
      48
  stratus:
    abbreviated, 11
    described, 48
    USWB photograph, 18
    weather, kind they precede,
      49
C$_M$, weather symbol, 67
CMH, 62
COD, 62
Code printer, 57
Code tables (*see* Weather maps,
  code tables)
Cody, Wyo.:
  station letters, 62
  station number, 62
Cold front (*see* Fronts, cold)
Cold wave, 108
Columbus, Ohio:
  station letters, 62
  station number, 62
Condensation process, 23-24
CPR, 62

Cumulonimbus clouds (*see* Clouds,
  cumulonimbus)
Cumulus clouds (*see* Clouds, cumulus)
CYS, 62

D$_C$, weather symbol, 67
DCA, 62
dd, weather symbol, 65
DDC, 62
Depression of dew point, defined,
  23
Des Moines, Iowa:
  station letters, 62
  station number, 62
Dew:
  continued fair indicated, 54
  how formed, 23
Dew point:
  defined, 22-23
  depression, 23
  how to determine, 24-26, 28-29
  table for determining, 26
DLH, 62
Dodge City, Kans.:
  station letters, 62
  station number, 62
DSM, 62
Duluth, Minn.:
  station letters, 62
  station number, 62

EKN, 62
Elkins, W. Va.:
  station letters, 62
  station number, 62
ELP, 61
El Paso, Tex.:
  station letters, 61
  station number, 61
ELY, 62
Ely, Nev.:
  station letters, 62
  station number, 62

ESC, 62
Escanaba, Mich.:
  station letters, 62
  station number, 62
EUG, 62
Eugene, Ore.:
  station letters, 62
  station number, 62
EUR, 62
Eureka, Calif.:
  station letters, 62
  station number, 62
Evaporation, 23

Fair weather cumulus, 49
FAR, 62
Fargo, N. D.:
  station letters, 62
  station number, 62
FAT, 62
ff, weather symbol, 65-66
Fog:
  advection, 108
  causes, 107-108
  formation, 23-24
  radiation, 108
  storms, when it precedes, 53
  weather maps, how indicated on,
    78
Forecasting:
  barometer and wind indications,
    51-52
  clouds, 46-50
  colder, 54
  fair, 54
  fair, continued, 54
  storm warnings, 53
  warmer, 55
  wind and barometer indications,
    51-52
Formulae:
  Centigrade to Fahrenheit, 22
  cloud speed, for determining,
    123
  Fahrenheit to Centigrade, 22

Fractocumulus clouds (see Clouds,
    fractocumulus)
Fractostratus clouds (see Clouds,
    fractostratus)
Fresno, Calif.:
  station letters, 62
  station number, 62
Fronts:
  cold:
    defined, 74
    discontinuities, 74-75
    formation, 84-85
    how to identify, 74-75
    precipitation, 94
  cold front occlusion:
    formation, 94
    precipitation, 94
  defined, 74
  forecasting:
    colder, 54
    fair, 54
    fair, continued, 54
    storms, 53
    warmer, 55
  neutral-type occlusion:
    formation, 95
    precipitation, 95
  occluded, defined, 74
  Polar, formation, 84-85
  stationary, defined, 74
  storm lines, 93-95
  surface, defined, 74
  upper air, defined, 74
  warm:
    cirrostratus clouds, 47
    cirrus clouds, 46
    defined, 74
    how to identify, 75-76
    precipitation, 94
  warm front occlusion:
    formation, 95
    precipitation, 95
  Washington weather map, 56
  weather map, how plotted on:
    cold, 74

Fronts (*cont.*):
  weather map, how plotted on (*cont.*):
    cold, high altitude, 74
    occluded, 74
    stationary, 74
    warm, 67
    warm, high altitude, 74

Galveston, Tex.:
  station letters, 61
  station number, 61
GJT, 62
Glaze, formation, 92
GLS, 61
Grand Junction, Colo.:
  station letters, 62
  station number, 62

h, weather symbol, 66
Hail, 105-106
Hair hygrometer, 28
HAT, 61
Havre, Mont.:
  station letters, 62
  station number, 62
Heat wave, 109
Helena, Mont.:
  station letters, 62
  station number, 62
HLN, 62
HON, 62
Humidity (*see* Relative humidity)
Huron, S. D.:
  station letters, 62
  station number, 62
Hurricanes, 106-107
HVR, 62
Hygrograph, 28-29
Hygro-thermograph, 28

iii, weather symbol, 65
IND, 62

Indianapolis, Ind.:
  station letters, 62
  station number, 62
Instrument shelter:
  building instructions, 112-114
  uses, 112, 114-115
International Morse Code:
  alphabet, 58
  numbers, 58
  punctuation, 58
  short wave broadcasts, 56
  special signals, 58
  speed, 58-59
INW, 62
Isobars (*see* Weather maps, isobars)

Jackson, Miss.:
  station letters, 61
  station number, 61
Jacksonville, Fla.:
  station letters, 61
  station number, 61
JAN, 61
JAX, 61

Kansas City, Mo.:
  station letters, 62
  station number, 62

LaGuardia Field, N. Y.:
  station letters, 62
  station number, 62
Las Vegas, Nev.:
  station letters, 62
  station number, 62
LBF, 62
LGA, 62
Lightning, 104
LIT, 62
Little Rock, Ark.:
  station letters, 62
  station number, 62

Long wave stations (*see* Radio range stations)
Louisville, Ky.:
station letters, 62
station number, 62
LSV, 62

Madison, Wis.:
station letters, 62
station number, 62
Maps (*see* Weather maps)
Mercurial barometer:
building instructions, 137-147
how it works, 34
temperature correction (*table*), 146-147
MIA, 61
Miami, Fla.:
station letters, 61
station number, 61
Millibars (*see* Barometric pressure, millibars)
Minneapolis, Minn.:
station letters, 62
station number, 62
MKC, 62
MSN, 62
MSP, 62

N, weather symbol, 65
Nashville, Tenn.:
station letters, 62
station number, 62
Nephoscope:
building instructions, 120-123
use, 19
Nₕ, weather symbol, 66
Nimbostratus clouds (*see* Clouds, nimbostratus)
North Platte, Nebr.:
station letters, 62
station number, 62

OAK, 62
Oakland, Calif.:
station letters, 62
station number, 62
Observation form:
reproduction, methods of, 8-9
sample, 9
what to include, 7-8
Occluded front (*see* Fronts, occluded)
OMA, 62
Omaha, Nebr.:
station letters, 62
station number, 62

PDT, 62
Pendleton, Ore.:
station letters, 62
station number, 62
Pikeville, Ky.:
station letters, 62
station number, 62
PIT, 62
Pittsburgh, Pa.:
station letters, 62
station number, 62
PKV, 62
pp, weather symbol, 67
PPP, weather symbol, 66
Precipitation (*see also* Rain and Snow)
cold front, 94
cold front occlusion, 94
glaze, 92
hail, 105-106
movement, general direction, 96
neutral-type occlusion, 95
sleet, 92
thunderstorm formation, 103-104
time of (*code table*), 69
topographical effect, 96
virga, 92
warm front, 93-94

Precipitation (*cont.*):
warm front occlusion, 95
Washington weather map,
shown on, 56
weather maps, how shown on,
78
Prefixes:
alto, 14, 16
fracto, 11
Psychrometer:
building instructions, 115-120
described, 24-25
how to use, 24-25
use, 24
PUB, 62
Publications:
CQ, 57
QST, 57
USWB base maps, 60
USWB Circular No. 235 (dew
point and relative humidity
tables), 25
Washington weather map, 56
"Weather, Astronomy and Meteorology," 13
Pueblo, Colo.:
station letters, 62
station number, 62

Radio (*see* Radio range stations
and Short wave stations)
Radio range stations:
altimeter setting, 80-81
broadcast schedule, 80
frequencies, 80
information broadcast, 80-81
Radiosonde, 97
Radio teletype, 57
Rain (*see also* Precipitation)
instrument for measuring, 38
rain gage:
building instructions, 147-151
described, 38

Raleigh, N. C.:
station letters, 62
station number, 62
RAP, 62
Rapid City, S. D.:
station letters, 62
station number, 62
RDU, 62
Relative humidity:
defined, 22
how determined, 24-25, 27-29
table for determining, 27
Reno, Nev.:
station letters, 62
station number, 62
RNO, 62
RR, weather symbol, 67
R$_t$, weather symbol, 67

s, weather symbol, 67
St. Louis, Mo.:
station letters, 62
station number, 62
Salt Lake City, Utah:
station letters, 62
station number, 62
SAN, 61
San Diego, Calif.:
station letters, 61
station number, 61
Saturation, 23
SDF, 62
SEA, 62
Seattle, Wash.:
station letters, 62
station number, 62
SGF, 62
Short wave stations:
frequencies, 59
WEK, 56
WSY, 56
Shreveport, La.:
station letters, 61
station number, 61

INDEX

SHV, 61
Sky coverage (*see* Clouds, sky coverage)
SLC, 62
Sleet, 92
Snow, how to measure, 38 (*see also* Precipitation)
Springfield, Mo.:
 station letters, 62
 station number, 62
Stationary front, 74
Station circle, 63
STL, 62
Storms (*see also* Thunderstorm)
 barometric pressure, 87
 hurricanes, 106-107
 origins in winter, 88
 paths in winter, 88
 tornadoes, 106
Stratocumulus clouds (*see* Clouds, stratocumulus)
Stratus clouds (*see* Clouds, stratus)
Surface front, 74
Symbols (*see* Weather maps, symbols)

Tallahassee, Fla.:
 station letters, 61
 station number, 61
T$_d$T$_d$, weather symbol, 65
Teletype, 57
Temperature:
 elevation, affected by, 82-83
 forecasting:
  fair, continued, 54
  storms, 53
 inversion, 83
 manuscript map, 56
 thunderstorms, affected by, 103
 Washington weather map, 56
 water, affected by, 84
Thermograph, 40
Thermometer:
 maximum, types of, 38-40

Thermometer (*cont.*):
 minimum, types of, 38-40
 mounting:
  instrument shelter, 111-115
  where, 21-22
 recording, 40
 thermograph, 40
Thunderstorms:
 air-mass, 102
 cold-front:
  frontal, 102
  postfrontal, 102
  prefrontal, 102
 formation, 103-104
 lightning, 104
 local, 102
 occluded-front, 103
 orographic, 103
 warm-front, 102
TLH, 61
Tornadoes, 106
TT, weather symbol, 66
Tucson, Ariz.:
 station letters, 61
 station number, 61
TUS, 61

Upper air front, 74
USWB:
 weather information, methods of distributing, 41-43
 observation times:
  auxiliary half-hourly, 43
  hourly, 43
  intermediate, 41
  primary, 41
  special, 43
 stations:
  code letters, 61-62
  code numbers, 61-62

Vapor pressure, 23
Virga, 47, 92

161

Visibility:
  defined, 20
  how to determine, 20
VV, weather symbol, 66

W, weather symbol, 66
Warm front (*see* Fronts, warm)
Washington, D. C.:
  station letters, 62
  station number, 62
Weather Bureau (*see* USWB)
Weather maps:
  air mass symbols, 78-79
  base:
    obtaining, suggestions for,
      60-61
    station circle, 63
    USWB, 56, 60
  code tables, 68-73
    barometric tendency, 71
    cloud amount, 70
    cloud direction, 69
    cloud height, 70
    cloud types, 68
    precipitation, time, 69
    weather, past, 71
    weather, present, 72-73
    wind velocity, 71
  fog, how indicated, 78
  fronts, how plotted, 67, 74
  high barometric pressure areas:
    isobars, 86
    wind direction, 86
  information supplied by, 56
  isobars:
    defined, 76
    function, 77
    how drawn, 76-78
    interpolation, 78
    sample map, 77
  manuscript, 56
  low barometric pressure areas:
    isobars, 86
    wind direction, 86

Weather maps (*cont.*):
  precipitation, how indicated, 78
  sample, changes in 24-hour pe-
    riod, 98-101
  symbols:
    sample form, 63-65
    transmission, order of, 64
  symbols (*table*):
    a, 67
    barograph trace characteris-
      tic, 67
    barometric pressure, 66
    C_H, 67
    C_L, 66
    cloud amount, 66
    cloud cover, 65
    cloud height, 66
    cloud movement, direction, 67
    cloud type, 67
    cloud type predominating, 66
    C_M, 67
    D_C, 67
    dd, 65
    dew point, 65
    ff, 65-66
    h, 66
    iii, 65
    N, 65
    N_h, 66
    pp, 67
    PPP, 66
    precipitation, amount, 67
    precipitation, time, 67
    pressure change, 67
    RR, 67
    R_t, 67
    s, 67
    snow depth, 67
    station number, 65
    $T_d T_d$, 65
    temperature, 66
    TT, 66
    visibility, 66
    VV, 66
    W, 66

Weather maps (*cont.*):
  symbols (*table*) (*cont.*):
    weather, past, 66
    weather, present, 66
    wind direction, 65
    wind speed, 65-66
    ww, 66
  transmission of information:
    code printer, 57
    newspapers, 55-56
    radio range stations, 80
    radio teletype, 57
    short wave radio, 56-59
    Washington weather map, 56
    WEK, 56-57
    WSY, 56
  Washington:
    information on, 56
    radiosonde, 97
  where obtained, 55-56
Weather, past, code tables, 71
Weather, present, code tables, 72-73
Weather symbols (*see* Weather maps, symbols)
Weather vane, building instructions, 124-130
WEK:
  broadcasting schedule, 56-57
  frequencies, 59
  radiosonde, 97
Wet bulb depression, 25
Williston, N. D.:
  station letters, 62
  station number, 62
Wind (*see also* Wind direction *and* Wind velocity):
  direction:
    high barometric pressure areas, 86
    low barometric pressure areas, 86

Wind (*cont.*):
  equator, flow from, 84
  poles, flow from, 84
  prevailing westerlies, 84
  velocity (*code table*), 71
Wind direction (*see also* Wind):
  defined, 30
  forecasting:
    colder, 54
    fair, 54
    fair, continued, 54
    storms, 53
    warmer, 55
  how expressed, 29
Wind vane, building instructions, 124-130
Wind velocity (*see also* Wind)
  anemometer, building instructions, 130-137
  Beaufort table, 32
  forecasting:
    colder, 54
    storms, 53
  how expressed, 30
  instrument for determining:
    described, 30-31
    building instructions, 130-137
Winnemucca, Nev.:
  station letters, 62
  station number, 62
Winslow, Ariz.:
  station letters, 62
  station number, 62
WMC, 62
WSN, 62
WSY:
  broadcasting schedule, 56
  frequencies, 59
  radiosonde, 97
ww, weather symbol, 66